Should We Mind the G

Gender Pay Differentials and Pu

Should We Mind the Gap?

Gender Pay Differentials and Public Policy

J. R SHACKLETON

iea

The Institute of Economic Affairs

First published in Great Britain in 2008 by
The Institute of Economic Affairs
2 Lord North Street
Westminster
London SW1P 3LB
in association with Profile Books Ltd

The mission of the Institute of Economic Affairs is to improve public understanding of the fundamental institutions of a free society, by analysing and expounding the role of markets in solving economic and social problems.

A CIP catalogue record for this book is available from the British Library.

ISBN 978 0 255 36604 5

Many IEA publications are translated into languages other than English or are reprinted. Permission to translate or to reprint should be sought from the Director General at the address above.

Typeset in Stone by MacGuru Ltd
info@macguru.org.uk

Printed and bound in Great Britain by Hobbs the Printers

CONTENTS

THE AUTHOR

J. R. Shackleton is Professor of Economics and Dean of the Business School, University of East London. He was formerly Dean of Westminster Business School and has taught at Queen Mary, University of London, and the University of Buckingham. Educated at King's College, Cambridge, and the School of Oriental and African Studies, he has also worked as an economist in the civil service. He has published widely in academic journals and written for several leading think tanks. He has given evidence to parliamentary committees, has appeared frequently on radio and TV, and has lectured in many countries. For the Institute of Economic Affairs he has written *Training Too Much?*, *Trouble in Store?* (with Terry Burke) and *Employment Tribunals*.

FOREWORD

The Equal Pay Act was perhaps the first manifestation in the UK of a new attitude towards employment that has developed from the 1970s onwards.

It is generally accepted that a civilised and prosperous market economy could not function if, for example, surgeons were paid the same as litter pickers. If they were paid the same, there would be a shortage of surgeons and nobody would wish to employ litter pickers. As F. A. Hayek noted in *The Road to Serfdom*, the end result of such central planning of wages would be to require a totalitarian state where central planners had to allocate individuals to jobs to overcome the mismatch between supply and demand. Such central planning would be illiberal and would also erode prosperity for reasons that are well understood.

For these reasons, most people accept that there will be wage differences for people doing different jobs but they argue that, when two different people do similar jobs, they should be paid the same. The reason why people doing different jobs are paid differently, however, is because of different conditions of supply *and* demand in relation to their jobs. As Alfred Marshall noted, price is determined by supply and demand together – in the same way as both blades of a pair of scissors cut the paper. To suggest that wages are determined by demand only is as fatuous as suggesting that only the top blade of a pair of scissors does the cutting. Yet those who suggest that the gap between the pay of men and women is caused only by employer discrimination are indeed suggesting that the wages of men and women are determined only by demand.

There may be legitimate reasons why employers wish to pay men and women differently. Discrimination for the sake of it is, however, highly unlikely. If women are paid less than men, why not make some men redundant and only employ women, thus increasing profits? One would expect this process to lead to a reduction in the pay gap – indeed, the process could go on until the gap was eliminated. If there really is a pay gap between men and women caused by discrimination then shareholders will pay a heavy price!

So, discrimination is not a good candidate for explaining the difference between the wages of men and women. Perhaps supply factors are more important.

The author of this monograph lucidly examines the evidence and finds that the free choice of men and women who are seeking employment – as well as earlier educational choices and the choices they make regarding their domestic arrangements – are at the heart of differences in pay levels. This conclusion is profoundly important. If we assume that the pay gap is caused by discrimination and, as a result, bring in yet more onerous regulations to add to the regulations that we already have, then we make the employment of both men and women more expensive. This will increase unemployment – especially among women – lower average wages and raise business costs. Indeed, it is proponents of anti-discrimination legislation, and not the classical economists who oppose it, who are treating women as mere economic units with no independent personal, non-economic preferences. If policies are enacted that close off options for women (or men) to enter lower-paid, part-time work at a convenient location, in jobs often chosen for social reasons rather than because they match the skills and experience of the applicant, then such women will either have no employment or will have to enter the world of formal, wage-maximising, full-time employment, which they may wish to avoid. By ignoring the supply side of the equation, those who would want to abolish wage differences end up ignoring the subjective preferences of all those who offer their services in the labour market.

There has been much further action following the Equal Pay Act to legislate away freedom of contract in the labour market. Some health and safety legislation, minimum holiday requirements, the minimum wage and even the regulations that prevent footballers' long-term contracts from being enforceable are all based on the false assumption that terms and conditions of employment are determined only by employers and not by both employers and employees to their mutual benefit. Professor Shackleton's monograph is a vital contribution to the debate not just on the so-called gender pay gap but, indirectly, on a whole host of other regulations that cause unemployment, depress wages and impose uniformity on a diverse population.

The author concludes that 'we should make far less of a song and dance about the gender pay gap'. This is certainly true, and the author's analysis proves his point convincingly. Perhaps we should even celebrate the pay gap as reflecting a labour market which, despite all the restrictions imposed upon it, manages to produce jobs that reflect the diverse talents and preferences of a heterogenous population.

The views expressed in this monograph are, as in all IEA

publications, those of the author and not those of the Institute (which has no corporate view), its managing trustees, Academic Advisory Council members or senior staff.

PHILIP BOOTH

Editorial and Programme Director
Institute of Economic Affairs
Professor of Insurance and Risk Management,
Sir John Cass Business School, City University
August 2008

ACKNOWLEDGEMENTS

The author is grateful for assistance and advice from Thalia Arygropoulos, David Henderson, Giorgio di Pietro, Clive Pritchard and Peter Urwin.

SUMMARY

- There is a sizeable gap between the average hourly earnings of UK men and women working full time: this is the gender pay gap. The gap has, however, declined over time and is expected to decline further given demographic trends and changes in women's qualifications. It could even go into reverse.
- The view that the UK has a particularly large gender pay gap by international standards is misleading. The gap is anyway only one indicator of women's economic status. Its size is not necessarily related to other indicators of sex discrimination and it can increase or decrease for reasons that have nothing to do with employers' behaviour.
- The pay gap may partly reflect compensating differentials: men's jobs may typically have disadvantages that are reflected in higher pay. Women report greater job satisfaction than men.
- There is little evidence of direct discrimination by employers against women. Discrimination is often inferred from the unexplained residual in econometric analyses of the causes of the gender pay gap.
- When attitudes and preferences, as well as objective characteristics such as work experience and qualifications, are brought into the picture, however, most of the pay gap can be explained without reference to discrimination.

- There is a larger gender pay gap for women working part time. These women tend to work in a narrow range of occupations; when this is taken into account the 'part-time penalty' shrinks to small proportions.
- Policies to reduce the gender pay gap seem unlikely to have much impact. The most significant policy, enforcing pay audits and equal pay reviews across the economy, could cause damage to the economic position of many men *and* women, and increase costs to business.
- There are other pay gaps which can be defined, by ethnicity, religious belief and disability, for example. Changes in the size of these gaps, and in more general measures of social inequality, may be in conflict with changes in the gender pay gap.
- Following from this, there is now so much variation in lifestyles and economic behaviour within the male and female populations that simple comparisons of average male and female pay are increasingly irrelevant.
- The conditions that would have to be met for a pay gap between men and women not to exist are impossible to achieve, although the gap can in principle be positive or negative.

TABLES AND FIGURES

Should We Mind the Gap?

Gender Pay Differentials and Public Policy

1 INTRODUCTION

The market economy continually creates jobs on which our prosperity depends. But it also creates a pattern of pay differentials which many of us dislike – whether it is low pay for those doing unglamorous but important jobs in our society, or very high pay for people who do not seem to contribute much. We complain about some older workers being poorly paid, or perhaps younger people should be better rewarded? Nurses and teachers should be paid more, many of us feel; footballers and City traders should be paid less. Some workers from minority ethnic groups do not seem to be paid as much as white workers, and people feel guilty and concerned about this. The list of worrying issues associated with pay can be extended indefinitely.

But the most discussed pay issue does not concern relatively small groups of the working population. Rather it concerns all of us, men and women. Ever since the Equal Pay Act was passed in 1970, the gender pay gap – loosely, the difference between male and female earnings – has been a major focus of attention in the UK. In the last few years policymakers' concern has increased. Despite a continuing fall over time in most measures of male–female differentials, the persistence of a pay gap disturbs many commentators.

The government-appointed Women and Work Commission claimed in 2006 that the UK's gender pay gap was among the largest in Europe and argued that women's work was being systematically undervalued because of occupational segregation. By removing barriers to working in more lucrative occupations and by increasing female participation in the economy, not only would social justice be promoted, but output would be increased by up to 2 per cent of GDP. More government action was called for.

The language of this debate can get very heated. Margaret Prosser of the Equality and Human Rights Commission has asserted that 'Women who work full-time are cheated out of around £330,000 over the course of their lifetime'. Similarly, the Fawcett Society asserts that 'women who work full-time are ripped off by £4,000 a year due to the pay gap'. TUC general secretary Brendan Barber says, 'It is completely unacceptable that ... women are still being paid less than men.' A TUC report makes the alarming claim that 'there is a cost to the economy of the underutilisation of women's skills in excess of £11 billion a year' (TUC, 2007).

And it isn't just the political left. Not to be outdone, the Conservative Party says that there is 'a strong business case for employers to ensure equal pay across the workforce', and argues for a range of new measures, including compulsory pay audits for those employers found by an employment tribunal to have discriminated (Conservative Party, 2007). There is already a requirement[1] that all public sector employers conduct such audits and develop measures to move towards equality. Many seek to extend this duty right across the economy.

---

1   Under the Equality Act 2006 the 'Gender Duty' requires public bodies to eliminate unlawful discrimination, including unequal pay, and promote equality of opportunity between men and women.

One such person is Ken Livingstone, the former London mayor. In the run-up to the recent mayoral election, reacting to a report on the pay gap in the capital, Mr Livingstone claimed that it would not be closed unless ministers introduced 'tough new laws'; failing this, there would be a 'serious impact on the future economic growth of the city'. His Liberal Democrat rival, Brian Paddick, declared that 'this pay gap isn't an anomaly, it's a disgrace'. He regarded Livingstone's comments as 'too little, too late', and suggested that the mayor had previously 'failed dismally to address the issue'. The eventual winner of the mayoral contest, Boris Johnson, was more circumspect, but even he felt it important to reiterate his belief that equal pay was a 'fundamental principle' that had to be strictly enforced.

Parliamentarians have also commented on the pay gap. Introducing a report from the Business Regulatory Reform Select Committee in February 2008, Judy Malabar, MP, spoke of the 'worryingly stubborn pay gap'. The Select Committee report called for further government action. Fear of such action had earlier led the usually strongly pro-market Institute of Directors to argue that the gap between the pay of male and female company directors was 'wholly unacceptable' and that companies needed to put their house in order if they were to avoid further regulation.[2]

In June 2008, the government responded to this climate of opinion by announcing its intention to develop further measures to promote equal pay in a forthcoming Equality Bill.

The UK is far from being alone in this concern. Most

---

2   http://press.iod.com/newsdetails.aspx?ref=308&m=2&mi=62&ms. The Institute of Directors normally defends the freedom of firms to set their own pay, but in this press release seems to want to stress that it feels it cannot justify gender pay differentials.

developed countries have some form of legislation covering sex discrimination and equal pay, in some cases much more strongly interventionist. Yet despite this, in almost every country men continue on average to earn more than women. The OECD has described this as evidence of 'under-utilisation of women's cognitive and leadership skills', and has claimed that 'at least 30% of the wage gap is due to discriminatory practices in the labour market'. In Europe, 'equal remuneration for equal work as between men and women workers' was enshrined in the Treaty of Rome.[3] But 50 years later, in July 2007, the European Commission reported the persistence of a large pay gap. This indicated 'an unacceptable waste of resources for the economy and society which prevents the productive potential of women from being fully realised'. Employment Commissioner Vladimir Spidla said that this was 'an absurd situation', necessitating changes to employment law and better application of existing law.[4]

Mr Spidla is in what is probably a very large majority of people who think that governments should do more. A poll conducted for the UK's Public and Commercial Services Union in early 2008 found that as many as 88 per cent of respondents believed it to be the government's responsibility to close the pay gap. So we have a strongly supported view that the market-generated pay differential between men and women is unfair and inefficient, and that governments have the power and the moral obligation to do something about it.

For many, these propositions are axiomatic and

---

3   In 1999 the narrowing of the gender pay gap was made part of the European Employment Strategy, reinforced in 2003 by a call for member states to formulate targets to narrow it.

4   BBC website: http://news.bbc.c.uk/2/hi/europe/6904434.stm.

unquestionable. They need closer examination, however. People in this country now broadly, if often reluctantly, accept that the free market is the best available way to organise economic activity. Belated realisation of this by the Labour Party was the basis of its electoral successes after 1997. So why exactly does the market apparently get things so badly wrong in relation to women's pay? And, if it does, can government redress things? It is not self-evident. Belief in the competence and efficiency of governments is at a very low level, and not only in this country. As already remarked, no government, anywhere, has succeeded in eliminating the pay gap – despite much time, money and energy being devoted to the cause. So what can governments actually do?

This paper spells out the key facts about the UK's gender pay gap and its development over time, looks at it in an international context, considers various explanations of the phenomenon and reflects on policies proposed to reduce or eliminate it. Ultimately the question we end up with is a controversial one: should we *really* mind the gap?

2 WHAT IS THE GENDER PAY GAP IN THE UK?

There are many 'pay gaps' that we could define and measure. To begin with, we must decide the relevant unit of comparison between men and women's pay. You might think we should take the gap in weekly, monthly or annual earnings as this is the way most of us think about our pay – but men work longer hours on average and so could legitimately be expected to be paid more, other things being equal. So hourly earnings are the most commonly used comparison. Because, for reasons discussed later, part-time hourly earnings are lower in the UK than full-time hourly earnings, comparisons are most commonly given between men and women who work full time. The Office of National Statistics (ONS) also prefers to use hourly pay excluding overtime, as overtime normally carries a premium and men work more overtime than women.

The big picture

These particular choices of indicator can be contested. So can the choice of which 'average' to take. International comparisons usually involve the mean, and this is certainly the most commonly quoted figure. On this basis, the UK's gender gap in hourly earnings[1] was 17.2 per cent in April 2007. This figure is frequently

---

1   Measured as mean male earnings minus mean female earnings, expressed as a percentage of mean male earnings: $[(E_m - E_f)/E_m]*100$. The data used are from the

Figure 1   The full-time gender pay gap in the UK

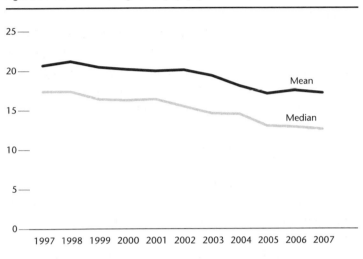

Note: See explanation in note 1. These figures are for full-time hourly earnings excluding overtime.
Source: Author's calculations from Office of National Statistics data

misunderstood, even by people who really should know better. For example, the *Financial Times* recently wrote[2] that 'men in full-time jobs are still paid on average 17% more than women in equivalent full-time posts'. Not so: women do different jobs from men

Annual Survey of Hours and Earnings (ASHE), which replaced the long-running New Earnings Survey in 2004. This survey uses a sample of employee jobs taken from HM Revenue and Customs PAYE records. This means the data are more reliable than in surveys that question employees directly: people are often hazy about what they earn. There is, however, little personal information to facilitate decomposition of the earnings gap, which we discuss later. So for some purposes we use other data sources, notably the Labour Force Survey, which questions households directly about pay but also asks many other questions about personal and job characteristics.

2   26 June 2008.

and the pay gap figure does *not* relate to identical employment, as we shall see.

Be that as it may, what has happened to the gap over time? It is difficult, in view of changes in data sources and sampling methods, to make exact comparisons, but the equivalent figure for the mean pay gap in 1970 was probably about 38 per cent. It has declined steadily if unspectacularly for many years, as illustrated for the last decade by Figure 1.

The mean does not necessarily convey the typical experience of participants in the labour market, however, as it is distorted by a small number of people with very high incomes, most of whom are likely to be male. An alternative measure is the median, the earnings figure below which half the sample population falls. This is the measure of the pay gap which the ONS prefers to quote: it was 12.6 per cent in 2007. As with the mean, the median gap was at its smallest recorded level.[3]

The mean and the median are what statisticians call 'measures of central tendency' – they give us some idea of the experience of people in the middle of the income distribution. But we shouldn't ignore the position at the extremities of the distribution: the pay gap for the bottom decile (the lowest-paid 10 per cent of the employed population) is about half that for the top decile (Connolly and Gregory, 2007). In general, changes that affect the extremities of the distribution will also affect the overall gender pay gap. So the introduction of the minimum wage, which disproportionately affected the pay of women,

---

3   This may seem a trivial point, but it matters when these figures are used rhetorically. In 1998, for example, the UK had the largest mean gender pay gap among nineteen OECD countries. Using the median measure, however, seven of these countries had larger pay gaps than the UK (OECD, 2002: 97).

probably contributed to the narrowing of the overall pay gap.

Other indicators are used in the gender pay debate. One area often highlighted is that of part-time earnings. While women's mean part-time hourly earnings are actually higher than those of male part-timers,[4] they are a small fraction of those of male full-timers. This version of the pay gap stood at 39 per cent in 2007, and unlike the other pay gaps mentioned so far, the part-time gap has shown little downward trend over time. Activists claim that women suffer a 'part-time penalty': this is much discussed in the academic literature and will be commented on later.

Variations

These highly aggregated measures conceal very considerable variations in the size of the pay gap from group to group within the population.[5] For example, the mean full-time pay gap in the private sector is much higher (at 22.3 per cent) than that in the public sector (13.6 per cent). This is not surprising given the much more compressed pay scales within the public sector, where the lowest pay tends to be well above the minimum wage and top executive and managerial pay is relatively modest by comparison with leading multinational companies. Variation between average male and female public sector pay is thus smaller, other things being equal. This implies that the higher the proportion of the workforce employed in the public sector, the lower is likely to be the economy-wide gender pay gap.[6]

---

4 Women part-time workers are typically older than male part-timers and are employed in a wider range of fields, including some high-paying ones such as professional occupations.

5 See Daniels (2008).

6 Women are much more likely than men to be working in the public sector. Over

This point is reinforced when looking across industries. Whereas the mean pay gap for those employed in education, almost entirely in the public sector, is 12.5 per cent, that in financial intermediation stood at 40.3 per cent in 2007.

Looking at variations between occupations, we see that the mean gap in 2007 was narrowest, at 7.3 per cent, for sales and customer service occupations and widest, at 26.8 per cent, for managers and senior officials. These figures should not surprise us, given the differences in the range of pay in different occupations. There are also big differences in the gender pay gap between regions. In 2007, the region with the largest median pay gap, 15.9 per cent, was the South-East, while the smallest was Northern Ireland at 2.8 per cent. These differences reflect the differing patterns of industrial and occupational employment in the regions.

Company size is also a factor. The median pay gap for companies with fewer than 25 employees was 12.4 per cent but rose to 18.4 per cent for those employing between 25 and 49 (Leaker, 2008).

Turning to personal characteristics, the most obvious point to make is that the pay gap differs with age.[7] It should be emphasised

a third of all female employees work in the public sector, compared with just 16 per cent of men (Platt, 2006).

7   It is always important to remember this; in all economies, pay bears a relationship to age. In the UK, women's earnings tend to peak in the 35–44 age group, while men's peak between 45 and 54. Failure to grasp this can lead to some confusion where changes in behaviour are occurring in younger age groups. An interesting example concerns 'anchors' on US television news programmes. One study found that on average male newscasters were paid 38 per cent more than females – a huge gender pay gap. But disaggregation showed that, within each age group, women were paid more than men. What was happening was that a large majority of young people (reflecting the gender composition of Communications and Media college courses) entering the job were women. These young

that in the younger age groups, 18–21 and 22–29, both mean and median measures of the gap are low; for 22–29-year-olds, the median gender pay gap was less than 1 per cent in 2007.[8] The gap rises with age, peaking in the 40–49 age group but remaining quite high until retirement age. This pattern combines both 'life-cycle' and 'cohort' effects. The first reflects the fact that the majority of 22–29-year-olds are actively pursuing careers. As they move into their thirties and forties, more of them are taking time out of the labour market to have families; when they return, it's often at lower pay relative to their male counterparts who have been continuously employed and will have progressed up the career ladder. Thus the pay gap widens over their working lives for men and women born in the same year.

There is also, however, a cohort effect as today's younger age groups of women are much better educated than their predecessors (girls and young women now clearly outperform boys and young men at school and university); they are delaying starting families; and they are spending less time out of the workforce when they do have children. This suggests that, as these groups age, the life-cycle effect will be less marked. The aggregate pay gap is likely to continue to decline, perhaps quite sharply.[9]

Something else worth flagging up is that there are variations in the size of the pay gap by domestic status. Single women earn as

---

women, on lower salaries, pulled down women's average pay relative to that of older men. 'Gender gaps and factors in television news salaries', www.missouri. edu/~jourVS/tvpaygo.html.

8   Indeed, data from the Labour Force Survey suggest that the median pay gap is actually negative for this age group – in other words, women in full-time employment earn more than men (Leaker, 2008).

9   The net result of the life-cycle and cohort effects will also depend on the relative size of different age cohorts.

much on average as single men, and indeed women in the middle age groups who remain single earn more than middle-aged single males. Moreover, a number of studies have established that, after controlling for relevant characteristics, married or partnered men earn markedly more than single men – although married women earn less than single females (Polachek and Siebert, 1993; Polachek and Xiang, 2006).

The fact that single men earn less than partnered men, other things being equal, is worth reflecting on. It is difficult to believe that employers discriminate against single men; this suggests that what we might call the 'partnered pay gap' is more likely to be caused by unobserved characteristics and attitudes of the different groups. Partnered men, with successes in the mating game, may be more confident and go-getting individuals. Or it may be that they attach more importance to building their careers if they have or intend to have a family. This is our first lesson: that pay gaps between groups are not necessarily the result of discrimination. We will frequently return to this point in different contexts.

As Table 1 shows, the addition of children intensifies differences in the pay gap[10] between different groups of men and women. Married men with children receive higher hourly pay, part of a picture where family responsibilities place a premium on the need for higher male earnings if, as is still usual, women take time out of the workforce. They also work longer hours: UK men with no children work an average of 42.9 hours a week, while those with a pre-school child work 47 hours. By contrast women

---

10   These figures are not strictly comparable with others quoted above as they are based on Labour Force Survey data: the ASHE does not include much information on the personal characteristics of individuals. The Labour Force Survey figures give a slightly lower estimate of the overall pay gap than that derived from the ASHE.

with no children work 38.3 hours; those with a pre-school child
25.4 (Paull, 2008).

Table 1 **Median hourly earnings and gender pay gap of full-time
working-age employees, April–June 2007**

	Median hourly earnings £ – male	Median hourly earnings £ – female	Gender pay gap %
All	10.70	9.47	11.5
Married/cohabiting/ partner	11.54	9.87	14.5
Single/widowed/ divorced/ separated	8.72	8.82	–1.1
No dependent children	10.23	9.41	8.0
1 dependent child	10.63	9.32	12.3
2 dependent children	12.49	10.63	14.9
3 dependent children	11.54	9.35	19.0
4 or more dependent children	11.22	7.24	35.5

Source: Labour Force Survey data, from Leaker (2008)

There is a final important point to make in this rapid sketch
of the stylised facts of the pay gap: we have to pay attention to
the ethnic heterogeneity of the male and female population of
this country. The UK now has a sizeable minority ethnic population, and generalising about 'men' and 'women' misses the fact
that different groups of women have very different labour market
experiences from each other, as do different groups of men. The
figures in Table 2 indicate that there are 'ethnic pay gaps' which
are at least as significant as the gender pay gap.

Table 2 **Mean hourly earnings and gender pay gap in full-time work, 2001–2005**

Ethnic group	Male earnings (£)	Female earnings (£)	Pay gap (%)
White British	11.59	9.65	16.7
Indian	12.45	10.28	17.4
Pakistani	9.32	8.31	10.8
Bangladeshi	7.05	8.94	−26.8
Black Caribbean	10.34	10.50	−1.5
Black African	10.17	9.38	7.8
All minority groups	11.07	10.07	9.0
All ethnic groups	11.57	9.73	15.9

Note: All earnings figures in 2005 £s
Source: Labour Force Survey data, calculated from Platt (2006)

This table gives further food for thought.[11] Notice in particular how it shows two ethnic groups where the gender pay gap is apparently reversed, with Black Caribbean men earning less than Black Caribbean women and Bangladeshi men getting less than Bangladeshi women. The main reasons for this are instructive for later analysis of the pay gap. Black Caribbean women are better qualified than their male equivalents; they do markedly better in school and university. Black Caribbean women are also more likely to be the sole household earner than is the case in other

---

11   In the paper by Platt (2006) from which these figures are taken, pay gaps are presented differently: they are all reckoned by comparison with white British males. This seems an odd approach, though perhaps revealing of the belief that white British males as a group are particularly privileged. In fact there are huge variations in the pay of white British men, many of whom are paid very badly. Note that men of Indian ethnicity earn markedly more on average than white British men.

ethnic groups; they are therefore likely to be more committed to advancing in the labour market. The issues with Bangladeshis are rather different. Bangladeshi women have a very low propensity to be in the workforce.[12] Those working in the labour market are likely to be disproportionately those who are more highly educated – doctors, teachers, pharmacists, for example – than the average Bangladeshi woman – and very likely more highly educated than the average working Bangladeshi man.

These examples show how analysis of the UK gender pay gap requires an understanding of quite complex interactions of culture, behaviour and labour market activity. They also illustrate that the 'headline' pay gap on which the media focus is only one indicator of women's labour market status and should be seen alongside data on their participation and employment. The examples also undermine the lazy assumption that women are an undifferentiated group suffering disadvantage in relation to a similarly undifferentiated group of men. The reality is far more subtle – as indicated, incidentally, by the fact that in 29 per cent of UK households women earn as much or more than their male partners (BERR, 2008: 11).

---

12   Over 70 per cent of UK working-age women of Bangladeshi origin are economically inactive.

3 INTERNATIONAL COMPARISONS

We noted that the UK appears to display a relatively large gender pay gap in relation to other countries. This needs to be qualified. There are considerable data problems when comparing different countries: for example, the ASHE method of using tax records would not be as reliable in countries such as Greece and Italy, where evidence suggests that there are high levels of tax evasion (European Commission, 2004). Nevertheless, comparisons are inevitable and other sources of data, normally Labour Force Surveys, which are conducted on a comparable basis across Europe, can be used. The most recent data for 2006, published by Eurostat, suggest that only Germany, Cyprus, Estonia and Slovakia among EU countries have a larger mean gender pay gap.[1]

But does this mean that women are getting a particularly raw deal in the UK? Not necessarily. For one thing, as discussed earlier, taking the median rather than the mean pay gap would alter the relativities between countries. We also need to be aware that the pay gap, a highly aggregated statistical measure, is driven by factors that are not immediately obvious to the casual observer. For example, one simple but important point to make is that you

---

1   All European countries show a 'raw' full-time gender pay gap. This gap has, however, been falling in size over time across the EU (European Foundation for the Improvement of Living and Working Conditions, 2006).

Figure 2   **Female labour force participation* and the gender pay
gap† in nineteen EU countries, 2006**

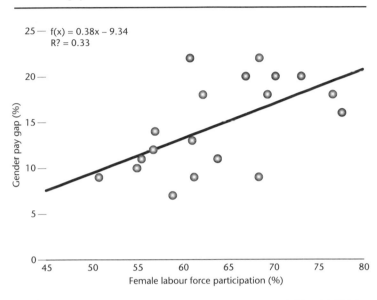

*Percentage of females aged 15–64 who are economically active. (Source: OECD)
†The figures used to calculate this are full-time gross hourly earnings; note that this is a slightly
different measure from that used in Figure 1 because of the need for comparability with data from
across the EU.
Source: Eurostat

have to be working before your pay enters the picture. There is
known to be a positive correlation between the female labour
force participation rate and the size of the gender pay gap (OECD,
2002), as illustrated in Figure 2.

Countries such as Italy and Spain, with low female participation rates, do not have the sort of flexible labour market that
makes it worthwhile for employers to incur the costs of taking
on low-skilled employees and for low-skilled workers to seek

highly taxed jobs. So most females who work in Spain and Italy are likely to be relatively highly skilled and educated; the others find it difficult or financially unrewarding to get work.[2] The consequence is that these countries' gender pay gaps are small, because they compare the earnings of men of all skill levels with those of a minority of relatively highly skilled females. By contrast, countries such as the UK, Germany and Denmark, which provide many opportunities for relatively low-paid work for women, exhibit larger gender pay gaps. Seen in this context, the pay gap should not be used in isolation to summarise a country's degree of gender equality or inequality – the same point we made in relation to Bangladeshi women in the previous chapter.

The point is further driven home by the Eurobarometer findings illustrated in Figure 3. Survey respondents across the European Union were asked in 2006 to say whether they believed sex discrimination in their country to be very widespread, fairly widespread, fairly rare or very rare. Italy and Spain, despite their modest pay gaps, were at the top of the league in terms of perceived discrimination, with 56 per cent and 55 per cent of respondents respectively saying it was fairly or very widespread in their country. By contrast the perception of discrimination in the UK was down at the EU average of 40 per cent, while Germany, despite having the largest gender pay gap among the major EU countries, reported an extremely low figure of 21 per cent (European Commission, 2007).

If the gender pay gap isn't a perfect indicator of a country's

---

2   To take an extreme example of this phenomenon from outside Europe: Bahrain appears to have a *positive* gender pay gap of around 40 per cent. That is, women on average earn much more than men. Very few women work, but they are concentrated in well-paid jobs (ITUC, 2008: 12).

Figure 3   The gender pay gap* and national perceptions of gender discrimination† in the EU, 2006

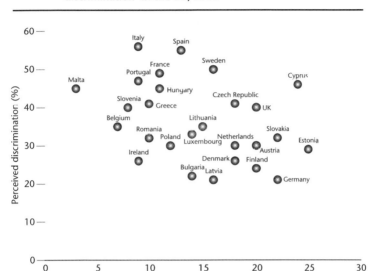

*Defined as in Figure 2.
†Percentage of population saying gender discrimination in their country is 'widespread' or 'very widespread'.
Source: Eurobarometer

gender equality, neither is a reduction in the gender pay gap an unambiguously good thing. Was it really a cause for celebration when in eastern Germany, after the Berlin Wall came down, there was a ten-point fall in the aggregate pay gap? For this was largely a consequence of the exit of large numbers of the less-skilled female workforce into unemployment or inactivity (Hunt, 2002). Or, to hypothesise something nearer home, would it be a bad thing if female labour force participation rose in the Bangla-deshi community – even though this would almost certainly tend to increase the gender pay gap, at least in the short run, as less-qualified women entered the workforce?

Many studies have looked for regularities in cross-country comparisons. Among other findings, it seems that the size of a country's gender pay gap is positively associated with its fertility rate, with the husband–wife age gap at first marriage, and the marginal rate of income tax.[3] These findings make sense when they are thought through. The higher the fertility rate, the greater the average number of children in a marriage or partnership, and the longer time a woman is likely to spend out of the workforce – meaning that on her return she is likely to have missed out on job progression and promotion opportunities, and may find her skills have depreciated. The higher the husband–wife age difference, the more likely it is that the husband will be earning more than the wife, and so the domestic division of labour will reflect this position, with men specialising in labour market activity and women focusing on domestic activity (any alternative allocation of labour tending to reduce the total household income). The higher the marginal tax rate, the less attractive it will be for women who expect to spend time out of the workforce to invest in education, training and other forms of human capital, and hence their earning power will be lower.

Finally, there seems to be some evidence of a negative association between the pay gap and the degree of compression of the wage structure.[4] Again this seems plausible: it is the same sort of principle which produces a smaller UK gender pay gap in the

3   Polachek and Xiang (2006).
4   Blau and Kahn (1992). But note that the OECD has recently commented that 'this appears to be essentially due to a few countries with wage dispersions far from the OECD average' (OECD, 2008: 147).

public than in the private sector, as mentioned earlier. The greater the spread of a country's earnings distribution,[5] the greater the possible size of its pay gap (while it is theoretically possible for the female and male earnings patterns to produce a large mean pay gap in an otherwise compressed distribution, this is unlikely as such patterns of earnings are rare).

International comparisons, therefore, suggest that the UK's gender pay gap is not uniquely large, and again emphasise that additional indicators are necessary in order to make proper comparisons. Variations in demographic factors as well as more narrowly economic considerations are relevant.

---

5 Many factors will shape the overall pay structure and thus the degree of compression. These will include the industrial structure and the extent of competition. Different collective bargaining regimes may also have an impact. In France, for example, where over 90 per cent of pay is collectively bargained for, unions clearly play more of a role in shaping the pay structure than in the UK.

4 THE LEGAL POSITION

Equal pay has been a feature of UK law since 1970, when the Equal Pay Act made it unlawful for an employer to treat men and women unequally in terms of pay and conditions, whether this was intended or not – although a five-year period of grace meant that this did not become operative until 1975. On joining the European Community (later the European Union) in 1973, the UK also signed up to European law, established under the Treaty of Rome, Article 119 (later Article 141) of which established the 'principle of equal remuneration for equal work as between men and women workers'. The adoption of European law strengthened UK legislative provision, as Article 141 adopts a rather wider definition of remuneration than the Equal Pay Act. As a consequence, it was a European Court of Justice ruling which brought pension schemes within the scope of pay equality.

The Sex Discrimination Act 1975 made unequal treatment unlawful in other aspects of employment, for example recruitment, promotion, transfer between jobs, training, redundancy and dismissal. All these factors, of course, have implications for pay and are thus relevant to the gender pay gap.[1] The Act

---

1 The Act, or later amendments, also covers such matters as sexual harassment at work – when action can be brought against fellow employees as well as employers. Trade unions can also be named where their practices are thought to be discriminatory. Various forms of potential discrimination outside the workplace – for example, in universities and schools, social clubs and places of entertain-

also established the Equal Opportunities Commission (EOC), tasked with monitoring the implementation of the law, advice on promotion of equal treatment of men and women and assisting complainants. The EOC, merged in 2007 with the Commission for Racial Equality and the Disability Rights Commission to form the Equality and Human Rights Commission, was for many years also a major propagandist for further extensions of equality.

The European Equal Pay Directive, incorporated without much enthusiasm into UK law by the Thatcher government in 1983, established that the principle of equal pay covers 'the same work or ... work to which equal value is attributed', a principle that has much wider implications for pay determination, for women have historically tended to work in different jobs from men. The concept of equal value, also known as 'comparable worth', is discussed later in this paper.

In the UK further legislation has promoted equality in the workplace, most recently through the Gender Equality Duty, which from 2007 has required all public authorities (vaguely defined, but going way beyond central government and local authorities to include the NHS, schools and universities) to promote gender equality and remove all remaining sex discrimination. In addition there is a right for employees to question their bosses about how their pay compares with others in the organisation doing similar work.[2]

---

ment, and in the provision of goods and services – are also covered.

2   A complainant can ask an employer for answers to specific questions about pay in a standard format. Employment tribunals can draw adverse conclusions from incomplete or evasive answers. In June 2008 the government announced that it would legislate to create further openness in pay. In a peculiar, though perhaps revealing, expression, Harriet Harman, Minister for Women and Equality, called this 'empowering the resentful' (*Financial Times*, 26 June 2008).

Equal pay claims

You can make a claim for equal pay by comparing your job with that of a member of the opposite sex ('the comparator') in three ways:

Like work

Your job must be the same, or broadly similar: minor differences will be examined to see whether they justify different pay.

Work rated as equivalent

A valid job evaluation scheme, compatible with the Equal Pay Act, has rated your job as equivalent to the comparator.

Work of equal value

Your job has not been evaluated, but (though it can be very different in nature) is claimed to involve the same level of skills as that of the comparator: an employment tribunal will appoint an independent expert to evaluate the job.

The comparator must be a person of the opposite sex. Note that men can claim equal pay with a better-paid female: though such cases are rare, they are not unknown. A comparator could be a predecessor (or a successor) in the same job role. He or she must be employed by the same or associated employers, though the full meaning of this has still to be established because of ambiguities between UK and European law. Comparisons can be made with different elements of a contract. For instance, you can make a case if, although your basic pay is the same as your comparator, you receive a smaller bonus.

An employer contesting a claim has to prove that the difference between your pay and that of the comparator results from a 'genuine material factor' other than gender. Such a factor cannot arise from indirect discrimination (e.g. the requirement to possess a particular qualification which is not strictly necessary and which one gender is less likely than the other to possess). Possible defences might include market conditions, movements up an incremental pay scale, previous job evaluations or pay protection under a 'red circling' arrangement – though in each of these cases tribunals and the courts have taken a narrower view over time as to what is a permissible defence.

A finding in your favour can lead to a rise in pay to that of the comparator, plus compensation in the form of back pay for up to six years.

Other legal initiatives with relevance to equal pay include maternity rights. The Employment Protection Act of 1975 first introduced statutory maternity pay and job protection for a limited period during maternity leave for women who had been with their employer for two years (full time) or five years (part time). A 1994 European Court of Justice decision extended rights to all women who have worked during pregnancy. The period of paid leave has been extended more than once – to 26 weeks in 2005 – and women can also take further unpaid leave and still retain job protection.[3]

There is also a right to take time off work for caring

---

3   Some limited paternity leave was introduced in 2003 but has been little used.

responsibilities and a right to request 'flexible working'. This was introduced by the Conservatives in the Employment Rights Act of 1996 and has since been extended. It is discussed later in the paper.

All these provisions are likely over time to affect pay by making it easier for women to retain their existing employment following childbirth. Women are therefore less likely to lose out by having time out of the workforce and possibly having to return at lower rates of pay (see Chapter 6).

5 EXPLAINING THE OVERALL PAY GAP

We have now established the salient facts about the UK pay gap, and the way in which it is subject to law. In this chapter various possible explanations for the differences in male and female earnings are examined.

We should begin by asking what determines pay, in general terms, in a competitive market. In such a market we would not expect everybody to earn the same. In the short run, wages are determined simply by supply and demand. If there is a sudden increase in the demand for construction workers because a new underground line is being built, and a limited supply of those with the necessary skills, wages will rise. But in the longer term, more workers will be attracted into construction, perhaps from abroad, or workers in other occupations will retrain. Longer term, it is possible that big pay differentials can persist if people possess unique skills or talents in high demand – Cristiano Ronaldo, Madonna or even Jonathan Ross. More controversially, high pay can be maintained if there are restrictions on entry into a field of employment. Sometimes this will be the result of legal barriers to entry into a profession – doctors or lawyers, for example – but it is often boosted by professional bodies or trade unions, which lobby for higher barriers to entry to protect their privileges.

Compensating differentials

Even where people are free to enter a well-paid field of employment, however, they may not choose to do so. Long ago Adam Smith, in his *Wealth of Nations*, spelt out several reasons why some workers consistently earn more than others. His reasoning forms the basis for the modern idea of 'compensating differentials' – where jobs that are unattractive may have to be rewarded with higher pay if they are to attract sufficient workers.

One factor is what Smith called 'the difficulty and expense' of learning a job. Some forms of employment require years of training, education and work experience – generically classed as human capital (Becker, 1993). The acquisition of human capital typically involves some cost to the trainee in terms of time and forgone earnings, even if the direct costs are paid by the state or the employer, and the worker will expect to be compensated by higher pay. This is clearly relevant to discussion of the gender pay gap, because women are likely to differ from men in relation to their human capital.

Note, however, that the amount of extra pay required will vary, Smith argues, with the 'agreeableness or disagreeableness' of the job. Apparently an academic job in a high-ranking research department at Oxford carries sufficient kudos to offset the higher salary obtainable in other universities (Booth et al., 2002). By contrast, a cook on a North Sea oil rig, for example, will normally be paid more than a similarly skilled cook working in a city. But whether a premium is paid, and its size, will depend on the tastes and preferences of individuals. If, over time, Oxford becomes overcrowded and less attractive as a city, the university will have to pay more to attract the best academics. If lots of cooks develop a taste for working at sea, their premium will diminish or disappear. This is pertinent to discussion of the pay gap, for women's preferences in relation to jobs may differ systematically from those of men, as we shall see.

It is rarely discussed in the debate over the pay gap, but part of the explanation for men's higher average pay could well be that there is a compensating differential for less attractive working conditions.[1] Men are more likely to work outside in all weathers. They are more likely to work unsocial hours.[2] Thirty-six per cent of male managers work more than 48 hours a week; the figure for women managers is only 18 per cent.[3] Men suffer much higher rates of industrial injury.[4]

Looking at the economy as a whole, we see that women's jobs are less at risk: in the three months from November 2007 to January 2008, there were 3.4 redundancies per thousand female employees; the figure for men was 5.3. Women are more likely to get employer-provided training: 13.6 per cent of females had received job-related training in the last four weeks in the third quarter of 2007, as against 11.3 per cent of males. They have a shorter commuting time to work (Women and Work Commission,

---

1   McNabb (1989) finds that, controlling for human capital variables, manual workers obtain a wage premium for inconvenient hours, job insecurity and unfavourable working conditions.

2   A larger proportion of men than of women work on Sundays, for example (Eurostat, 2008: 86).

3   Note that men do not work less overall, including domestic work, than women – despite popular belief. National Time Use surveys indicate that men aged 25–44 spend slightly more time in total in work, both paid and unpaid, than women (ibid.: 111).

4   In 2006/07, men were two and a half times more likely than women to suffer a major injury at work. Davies et al. (2007) find evidence for a significant compensating pay differential for the risk of major accidents in, for example, process, plant and machinery occupations in the UK. Grazier (2007) finds a similar result for risk of death across a wider section of the employed population.

2006) and take more time off work. No wonder, perhaps, that they report greater job satisfaction than men (Booth and van Ours, 2008).

The implication of this is that the 'true' gender pay gap may be less than the measured one, as male pay may include an element of compensation for less attractive working conditions. This is ignored in many empirical studies and it is a serious omission.

Discrimination

Discrimination is often seen as an important explanation of the gender pay gap. The concept needs some clarification before we assess this belief.

Discrimination is a word that has changed its common meaning. Whereas once it was seen as something worthy of praise – as in somebody displaying 'a fine discrimination' between paintings or pieces of music – it now usually means something unfair, unacceptable and, in an increasing number of cases, illegal.

Economic analysis of the subject effectively began with the work of Gary Becker in the 1950s (Becker, 1957). In Becker's analysis, employers, fellow employees and governments may engage in discrimination, which he interprets as an economically unjustified preference for one group over another, such that members of the favoured group would be more likely to be given a job, to be paid more, or otherwise treated better than another group or groups. Becker's particular insight was that this preference, this 'taste for discrimination', could be seen as an end in itself, something that therefore entailed a 'cost' to the discriminator. For example, employers might prefer to hire male rather than female workers even if this were more expensive. In this respect Becker differed fundamentally from Marxists and other critics of capitalism who saw discrimination as a means of exploiting subordinate groups to the benefit of the discriminator.

If this taste for discrimination exists, it *may* be manifested in the existence of a pay gap. This is not necessarily the case, however. If rigorous laws prevent women being paid less than men, discriminating firms may simply hire fewer women, but they will be paid the same as men. So Becker's analysis supports the point made earlier in relation to Italy and Spain: the size of the pay gap in itself does not say very much about the extent of discrimination.

From Becker's analysis, originally applied to racial differences, it followed that discriminating firms would hire white workers, or pay them a higher wage, rather than black workers of identical or superior productivity characteristics. But, he reasoned, this behaviour would raise costs. If other employers who were 'colour-blind' entered the market, they would be able to undercut the discriminators and gain a competitive edge.

From this, Becker argued that, in a competitive market where non-discriminators were free to enter, discrimination would be unlikely to persist for long.[5] It could be found where firms had monopsony power;[6] it could also be found where trade unions exercised power to protect white workers against blacks, or, in our

5   Unless, as the OECD points out (2008: 151), discriminators differed systematically from non-discriminators in other ways that favoured their competitiveness – for instance, displaying greater entrepreneurial ability. But there seems no obvious reason to suppose this to be the case.

6   Where a firm is the dominant employer in an area, it may be able to segment the job market and pay different rates to different groups of workers without being undercut by other firms. Such a situation could also arise if gender segregation occurred as a result of employee job choice.

context, men against women.[7] But Becker, as a Chicago economist, argued that market power to sustain discrimination is unlikely to persist for any extended period if free entry of firms is allowed and union power is limited. Therefore any sustained discriminatory power is to be attributed to government interference in the free market. Apartheid South Africa is an obvious example. And in the USA, the so-called 'Jim Crow' laws in the South sustained labour market discrimination for many years: when they were abolished there was a big increase in the relative pay of black workers – the reduction in the white/black pay gap since then has been relatively modest (Epstein, 1992).

In our current context, it should be remembered that government discrimination against women was often quite explicit in the UK until the mid-twentieth century, with different pay rates for men and women civil servants and teachers, requirements to resign on marriage, and prohibitions on working at all in certain jobs.

A quite different approach to the economics of discrimination was taken by Arrow (1972) and Phelps (1972). In their view, employer discrimination was not the result of 'tastes' or simple prejudice. Rather, it was a rational response to imperfect knowledge about the characteristics of individual job applicants. This led risk-averse employers to operate with stereotypes, which

---

7   There are certainly many instances in the past where unions have implicitly or explicitly protected groups of male workers against 'dilution' by females, and where the demand for a 'family wage' focused on the male as household head. There is some evidence from both the UK and Australia that the decline in union strength since the 1970s is statistically associated with the decline in the gender pay gap (Bell and Ritchie, 1998; Preston, 2003). More generally, to the extent that unions protect 'insiders' from 'outsiders', and women are more likely to fall into the latter category, they may exacerbate the pay gap.

might be accurate or inaccurate, of common group characteristics. Suppose – and this is true, whatever its cause – that women on average take more time off work than men for sickness, employers might hold this against a female job applicant even if, unknown to the employer, she as an individual had a low sickness risk. Such 'statistical discrimination' would be economically rational even if unfair to individuals in particular cases.[8]

As in Becker's reasoning, however, free competition ought to reduce discrimination. Some firms might find it easier than others to acquire more information about individuals, or would be prepared to take a chance on them, because they faced different cost and demand conditions. Not all firms, therefore, will behave in the same way. Furthermore, individuals are not passive. They can signal more information about themselves and market themselves more effectively to potential employers. One way they could in principle do this is to offer to work for less pay during a trial period. In most developed countries, however, such trial arrangements are difficult if not impossible because of legislation on equal pay, minimum wages and employment protection. Again, governments may be part of the problem.

Some support is given to the common Becker and Arrow/ Phelps thesis that free competition tends to eliminate discrimination, while some forms of government intervention assist it, by a paper by Polachek and Xiang (2006). These authors find that

---

8   It is possible to develop more sophisticated versions of statistical discrimination in multi-stage career models. For example, Bjerk (2008) shows that equally skilled workers from different racial or gender groups will have different probabilities of accessing top jobs in organisations depending on differences in average skill levels, the precision with which they can signal their skills prior to entering the labour market, and the frequency with which they can signal their skills before entry.

countries with greater economic competition, as measured by the Economic Freedom Index, display lower gender pay gaps. The OECD has recently reached similar conclusions, with the added insight that product market regulation may be an important factor, by protecting disproportionately male 'insiders' from new entrants. It finds that 'regulatory barriers to competition explain between 20% and 40% of the cross country/time series variation in the gender wage gap' (OECD, 2008: 161).

As overt discrimination is now illegal, direct evidence of its existence is hard to come by. Some studies have used 'correspondence tests', where there is some limited evidence that matched job applications from females and males elicit more interview offers for males. Another example is that of 'blind' musical auditions which suggest women do better if only their playing is heard.[9] And careful documentation of practices in, for instance, construction indicates prejudice against female employees.[10] But this sort of evidence is sparse.

Those seeking evidence of discrimination might also point to the large number of employment tribunal cases over sex discrimination and equal pay issues as evidence of the problem. It is certainly true that the number of such cases has risen recently: between 2004/05 and 2006/07, the number of sex discrimination cases accepted by tribunals rose from 11,726 to 28,153, while equal pay cases rose from 8,229 to a massive 44,013. There has been little detailed analysis of the growth of these cases, but it is known that there were special factors associated with changes in

---

9   Goldin and Rouse (2000) find that women orchestral musicians are significantly more likely to be hired when they are auditioned behind a screen so that their gender is hidden.

10   Clarke et al. (2004).

the law, and with the advent of 'no-win, no-fee' lawyers. It is interesting, incidentally, that a disproportionate number of these cases are against public sector employers,[11] although as we have seen the gender pay gap is much smaller in the public sector. The majority of these claims were multiple claims brought against local authorities and the NHS, paradoxically as a result of the introduction of Job Evaluation Schemes aimed at closing the pay gap. This is discussed in a later chapter.

Looking at the private sector, though, it is clear that only a small proportion of equal pay and sex discrimination claims succeed. The Women and Work Commission examined all private sector equal pay claims from 2000 to 2004 and found that only 25 reached the decision stage, with applicants winning in only five cases.

Despite their growing numbers, tribunal cases are brought by only a tiny proportion of the workforce and cannot really do much to explain the aggregate phenomenon of the overall gender pay gap. They often concern procedural issues rather than more fundamental matters: in the case of sex discrimination tribunal claims they are often about issues such as sexual harassment, bullying and other offences rather than issues directly related to pay.

Econometric analysis of the pay gap

Given the limited evidence of direct discrimination, in trying to analyse pay inequality researchers have increasingly concentrated

---

11 Voluntary sector employers are also over-represented among tribunal respondents.

on econometric work.[12] A substantial literature is concerned with separating out that part of the overall gender pay gap that can be accounted for by relevant economic characteristics[13] and that residual part which could possibly be attributable to discrimination – defined as paying different amounts to men and women for identical skills and abilities, and usually seen as conscious or unconscious behaviour by misguided employers.

The large number of studies that have been made of pay gaps in many different countries vary considerably in methodology and conclusions, but there are some common threads. Most studies use a statistical technique first developed more or less simultaneously by Oaxaca and Blinder (Oaxaca, 1973; Blinder, 1973). This decomposes the gender pay gap into two parts. The first component is the difference in pay associated with differences in observable characteristics such as experience and education. The second is the 'residual', which may partly result from discrimination.

The procedure involves first estimating a wage equation,[14] which relates the logarithm of wages to years of education, work experience and a range of other productivity-related characteristics that are available in the particular dataset the researcher is using. In effect the coefficients of the estimated equation indicate how much the labour market pays for these characteristics. One equation may be estimated for males, and then the regression coefficients are used to calculate what women would have earned had their characteristics been rewarded at the same pay rate as

---

12 Econometrics uses statistical methods to analyse and test relationships between economic variables.

13 Such as those which we saw in Chapter 2 to be associated with variations in the size of the pay gap.

14 Usually called a 'Mincerian' function after Jacob Mincer, who developed this technique, first pioneered by Becker and Chiswick (1966).

men. This typically reduces the pay gap between men and women quite significantly, leaving the 'unexplained' element as the differences in returns to productivity-related characteristics for males and females.[15]

Another wage equation may be estimated from data on women's earnings; the coefficients in this regression can then be applied to see what men would have earned if their characteristics had been paid at the same rate as those of women. This can then be used to give another possible estimate of the proportion of pay explained by worker characteristics, together with the residual potentially attributable to discrimination. Alternatively a pooled regression may be used (Neumark, 1988).

Since the early studies, more sophisticated modelling has developed. One problem with the Oaxaca–Blinder approach is sample selection bias. When calculating the gender pay gap, researchers are using data on men and women who are in employment. Many women, however, especially those with lower levels of skills and qualifications or with less interest in careers, may drop out of the workforce and live on benefits and/or intra-household transfers from partners. So women who work may be untypical of all women – they are the more skilled and committed females,

---

15   Another way to describe this, as set out by Harkness (1996), is as follows:
     The logarithm of the wage is determined by
     (1) $\log w_m = b_m X_m$ for men, where X_m is a set of productivity-related characteristics and b_m the coefficients on these characteristics
     (2) $\log w_f = b_f X_f$ is the corresponding equation for women
     (3) The pay gap then becomes: $\log w_m - \log w_f = (b_m - b_f)X_m + b_f(X_m - X_f)$.
     The first term on the right-hand side is the difference in returns to the characteristics for men and women, while the second term represents differences in the means of male and female characteristics (e.g. years of work experience). The first term is the unexplained difference in returns which is often casually attributed to 'discrimination'.

while employed men will cover a far wider spectrum of ability and commitment. The size of the underlying wage gap – between what men and women could earn – may therefore be underestimated, and the statistical explanation of the gap erroneous. The 'Heckman correction' gets round this problem by using other variables to estimate the probability of employment of men and women, and uses this as a further explanatory variable in the wage equation (Heckman, 1979).

Other refinements have involved the development of international comparisons through the Juhn, Murphy and Pierce methodology (Juhn et al., 1991). This approach assumes an 'institutionalist' view that the structures of pay (including collective bargaining systems) affect gender differentials. It involves decomposing down cross-country differences in the gender pay gap by taking one country as a benchmark, and analysing pay gaps in other countries with reference to the pay structure of that country. So the decomposition involves explaining differences in pay gaps by reference to gender differences in observed characteristics, to a component associated with cross-country differences in wage structures and to an unexplained element. Some interesting work has been done with this approach (OECD, 2002: ch. 2).

It is worth emphasising again that analysts are not unanimous in their choice of modelling strategy.[16] And the quality and coverage of the data used in different studies often leave much to be desired. While most studies suggest that there is a sizeable unexplained residual pay gap, this varies considerably in size, as does the proportion of the explained gap associated with relevant individual and job characteristics.

16   See Grimshaw and Rubery (2002) for a critique of the Oaxaca–Blinder and subsequent approaches.

A rather different approach to decomposition is used in work done by Wendy Olsen and Sylvia Walby for the Equal Opportunities Commission. As this has been widely quoted in UK debates, it is worth describing in some detail. Olsen and Walby adopt a novel approach which avoids some of the problems they perceive with the Oaxaca–Blinder technique. They prefer to estimate a single equation for men and women which produces estimates of coefficients on a range of explanatory variables. They then bring out the sizes of the main components of the pay gap by 'simulating the hypothetical changes which would be needed to bring women's levels of these components into line with those of men' (Olsen and Walby, 2004: 24). They use data from the British Household Panel Survey (BHPS),[17] and their results are summarised in Table 3 overleaf.

How does their approach work? Their wage equation shows a significant relationship between hourly earnings and, for example, the proportion of men in an occupation. This proportion is an indicator of 'gender segregation' at work,[18] which is believed by many to be an element in perpetuating pay inequality. The coefficient on this variable is 0.13, which means that, other things being equal, pay rises by 1.3 per cent for every 10 per cent more males in an occupation. So Olsen and Walby simulate the effect of increasing the proportion of men in every female-dominated

---

17 The BHPS has a good deal of information about work history, family commitments and so on, and is thus a useful data source. Estimates of the aggregate 'raw' pay gap from the BHPS are similar to those from the more widely used NES/ASHE and the Labour Force Survey.

18 If de facto segregation exists it is theoretically possible for employers to discriminate between men and women in setting pay, though it is unclear why this possibility would itself generate a pay differential. Such a differential is likely to reflect other factors such as lower turnover associated with relative geographical and occupational mobility, which are supply-side, or employee, characteristics.

occupational category to 50 per cent. This is what they mean by an 'unsegregated' workforce. If this were to be done, they find, earnings in these categories would rise by an average of 2.5 per cent, or about 10 per cent of the measured pay gap in their study.

Table 3 **Decomposing the gender pay gap in Great Britain, 2002**

Factors associated with GB gender pay gap	%
Women have less full-time work experience	19
Interruptions to female employment (childcare, etc.)	14
Gender segregation (concentration of women in female-dominated occupations)	10
Education (older women have less education than males)	8
Institutional factors such as firm size (women tend to be in smaller firms) and union membership	8
Years of part-time working (women have more part-time work experience: this has a negative effect)	3
'Being female' (unexplained, possibly discrimination and preferences/motivation)	38
TOTAL	100

Source: Olsen and Walby, 2004

This careful study still shows a largish 'unexplained' pay gap, although it's a good deal smaller than some earlier studies, where only tiny proportions of the gap were explained (Connolly and Gregory, 2007: 165). The large size of the unexplained gap in some of these studies is often the result of poor or proxy data. For example, work experience is used in estimating wage equations, but information on work history is often missing or incomplete and some studies use the difference between current age and age at (assumed) completion of schooling as a proxy for this. For many women, and some men, with periods

Table 4 **Subjects studied in higher education by UK women, 2006**

Women are over-represented (> 58.9%)	% of students who are female	Women are under-represented (< 58.9%)	% of students who are female
Subjects allied to medicine	82.7	Medicine and dentistry	58.4
Education	75.5	Mass communication and documentation	56.4
Veterinary science	74.9	History and philosophical studies	55.0
Languages	68.0	Business and administrative studies	49.7
Social studies	64.2	Physical sciences	41.6
Biological sciences	63.9	Mathematical sciences	37.2
Combined studies	61.9	Architecture, building and planning	29.1
Agriculture and related subjects	61.2	Computer science	21.7
Law	60.5	Engineering and technology	15.0
Creative arts and design	60.2		

Source: Derived from Higher Education Statistics Agency data

outside the workforce, this will exaggerate the true extent of their work experience. This in turn will lead to the role of experience in explaining the pay gap being underestimated because the differential in experience between men and women is inaccurately measured. Moreover, another key explanatory variable in wage equations, education, is often just measured by years of schooling, when it is known that the type and especially the subject of qualification are important, particularly in higher education. Women tend not to study the same subjects as men at university, as Table 4 shows. Overall, in 2006, women accounted for 58.9 per cent of the UK student population, but the proportion of women in the major subject areas shown varies considerably. Women are startlingly under-represented in some subjects and over-represented in others.

This in itself might not matter if different subjects were rewarded equally in the labour market, but this is not the case. For example, a study for the Royal Society of Chemistry (Pricewaterhousecoopers LLP, 2005) showed that individuals' rates of return on more narrowly defined degrees varied widely. Engineering, chemistry and physics, where women are seriously under-represented in the student population, offer rates of return significantly above average. By contrast, psychology degrees (where almost 80 per cent of the 66,000 students in 2006 were female) and linguistics, English literature and Celtic studies (where 72 per cent of over 70,000 students were female) give returns that are markedly less than the average.

Variations in rates of return might reflect discrimination or the systematic undervaluing of the jobs of graduates in areas where women dominate. But there are some obvious structural factors at work. One is the sector in which different types of graduates are likely to work. Over a quarter of all women in higher education are studying nursing or education. The vast majority of graduates in these areas will work in the public sector: there are relatively few highly paid jobs in government employment.

Lifestyles, preferences, attitudes, expectations

After allowing for these factors, is that part of the pay gap left unexplained attributable to discrimination, as many claim? Well, possibly, but in addition to the type of factors listed in Table 3 there is also what econometricians call 'unobservable heterogeneity'. Here this means differences in attitudes, preferences and expectations which can cause apparently similarly qualified and experienced individuals to behave very differently.

Catherine Hakim, a sociologist whose work on 'preference theory' has created some controversy, claims that, in countries such as the UK, women now have a wide range of lifestyle options[19] and that they can be classified into three relatively distinct groups by their preferences – those who are home-centred, those who are work-centred and those who are 'adaptive'.

The first group, which she estimates to be approximately 20 per cent of UK women, prioritise family life and children, and prefer not to work in the labour market (though they do so, they are not career-driven). Work-centred women, again about 20 per cent, are likely to be childless, committed to their careers and with a high level of investment in qualifications and training. The largest group, the 'adaptives', around 60 per cent of UK women, want to work, but they also want families. Their careers tend to be more erratic.[20]

Hakim carried out a national survey which indicated that women's expressed preferences were good predictors of their employment status, whereas, perhaps surprisingly, their educational qualifications were not: some well-qualified women were in

---

19 Hakim argues that there have been major changes in society and the labour market, producing a 'qualitatively different' set of options and opportunities for women. These changes she identifies as the contraceptive revolution, the development of sex discrimination and equal opportunities legislation, the expansion of white-collar and service occupations, the creation of jobs for secondary earners, and the increasing importance of lifestyle choices in affluent societies (Hakim, 2000).

20 According to Hakim, these groups are found in all developed economies, although the proportions may differ from country to country.

the 'home-centred' camp. She argues that her preference theory 'explains continuing sex differentials in labour market behaviour (workrates, labour turnover, the choice of job etc) and hence also in the pay gap' (Hakim, 2002: 1).

Hakim's assertion receives some support from the work of Arnaud Chevalier (2004; 2007), who uses data on attitudes and expectations to demonstrate how standard econometric analysis of the gender pay gap often misleads by leaving a large unexplained pay gap which is then too easily attributed to discrimination.

His work is based on a survey that covers more than 10,000[21] UK graduates who left university in 1995 and provides data on the 42 months following graduation. Unusually, in addition to information on wages, educational attainment and job history, it provides data on family background, subject of degree and, most importantly, attitudes and expectations. The survey asked twenty questions, coded on a five-point scale, about character traits, motivation and expectations.

The data indicated a mean raw gender pay gap of 12.6 per cent for this group of young graduates. Chevalier's meticulous multi-stage process illustrates very clearly that the large residual pay gap found in many studies is likely to be the result of model misspecification because of the omission of explanatory variables.

What Chevalier does is fascinating. In essence he recapitulates the development of work on pay gaps in various stages, to show how adding information about individuals can explain more and more of the difference in earnings. His first step is to use a very basic specification using labour market experience,

---

21 Although, because of the focus of his study on full-time employees and the need to eliminate incomplete data, his econometric analysis draws on just over five thousand records.

age at graduation, ethnicity and region of residence as explanatory variables. Many widely cited studies of gender pay gaps tend to be confined to a few variables such as these. As might be expected, given that the group is fairly homogeneous in view of them having a degree and being relatively young, the simple model explains very little, only about 20 per cent, of the observed pay gap between men and women.

He then goes on to include further explanatory variables such as A-level score, degree results, type of higher education institution and postgraduate qualifications. These indicators add a little, but not very much, to the explanatory power of the model. Adding in controls for the subject in which these young people graduated, however, increases the explanatory power of the model very significantly, with over 50 per cent of the pay gap now accounted for.

A further iteration extends the model to include other objective data such as the characteristics (size and sector) of the workplace, the type of contract, and the 'feminisation' of the occupation. This raises the proportion of the wage gap which is explained to 65 per cent. The addition of data on the number of jobs held since graduation – a measure of mobility – adds another minor increment to the specification's explanatory power.

The final specification includes information on the values that graduates attach to jobs and their career expectations. Men and women differ significantly with regard to these characteristics: men are more likely to state that career development and financial rewards are very important, and are much more likely to define themselves as very ambitious, while women emphasise job satisfaction, being valued by employers and doing a socially useful job. Two-thirds of women in this sample expect to take career breaks for family reasons; 40 per cent of men expect their partners to do this, but only 12 per cent expect to do it themselves.[22]

When these attitudinal variables are added to the specification, the result is that 84 per cent of the wage gap can now be explained. This suggests that many of the models that generate large 'unexplained' wage gaps, and from which non-specialists frequently infer a significant element of employer discrimination, are simply misspecified. They just don't incorporate sufficient explanatory variables for a satisfactory analysis of the causes of the gender pay differential.[23]

How exactly do these attitudes and values lead to women being paid less than men? One way is through different individuals' choices of potential employers. A recent survey of young graduates shows that women's choices of preferred employers are very different from those of men (Trendence, 2008). Of the top 25 ideal employers for women, twelve were in the public or voluntary sectors, as against only four out of 25 for men. The top three ideal employers for women graduates were all in the public sector.

Such preferences mean that many bright women are deliberately choosing jobs where really high earnings are impossible or unlikely. They clearly regard other aspects of the job – a greater sense of moral purpose, perhaps? Or maybe greater job security,

---

22 In every country men typically marry/partner women who are younger than them, and are therefore likely to be earning less for that reason alone. As pointed out previously, if having children requires at least one parent to spend time out of the workforce, economic logic would dictate that the partner with the greater earning power should continue in employment – and indeed, as the evidence mentioned earlier suggests, even increase their hours of work and effort.

23 Other studies also report relevant psychological differences between men and women, for instance in relation to self-esteem, risk aversion, attitudes to competition and career orientation (Manning and Swaffield, 2008).

less stress and relatively generous pension provision[24] – as offsetting the reduced chance of very high earnings. This is the compensating differential principle touched on earlier.

Another way in which employee attitudes influence earnings outcomes may be through different approaches to pay negotiations and promotion applications. Particularly at more senior levels, the pay offer an employer makes may be negotiable – if, that is, the employee chooses to negotiate. In their book *Women Don't Ask: Negotiation and the Gender Divide*, American academics Linda Balcock and Sara Laschever claim that women are very reluctant to negotiate over salaries. In one US study eight times as many men as women graduating with master's degrees negotiated their salaries, adding an average of 7.4 per cent to their starting pay. This initial gap is likely to persist and grow over time. This is partly because women may have lower expectations: Balcock and Laschever (2003) report a study suggesting women's salary expectations for their first job are significantly lower than those of men going for similar jobs.

In the UK, an analysis of the pay gap among academic economists indicates that men receive more promotions and higher placings on pay scales, and one of the factors associated with this is the receipt of outside offers. Men receive more outside offers than women and are thus able to negotiate their pay upwards (Booth et al., 2002). They also make more pay-oriented moves between jobs than women.[25]

---

24 Pension provision is a very important element of the total remuneration package in many parts of the public sector – teaching, for example, where employer contributions are substantial and add 20–25 per cent to 'real' earnings. Indeed, researchers have suggested that public sector pensions are worth about twice the official contribution rates (see Record, 2006).

25 Manning and Swaffield (2008) report that 47.1 per cent of men leaving early-

So the conclusion we can draw from empirical analysis of the full-time pay gap is that a high proportion of this gap can be accounted for, given sufficient information on individual and job characteristics and the attitudes and expectations of employees. Males and females make different choices in the labour market, in terms of the trade-off between pay and other job characteristics, choice of education, choice of occupation and attitudes to work. These strongly influence earnings. Employer attitudes and discrimination seem not to be nearly as important as politicians and lobbyists have suggested.

career jobs do so either because they are promoted or moving to a better job; only 43.6 per cent of women leaving such jobs do so for financial gain.

6 THE PART-TIME PAY GAP

But does this conclusion also hold for part-time workers,[1] where the overwhelming majority is female and the pay gap is much larger and shrinking more slowly?

The situation does look rather different with part-timers. For example, work experience is normally assumed to add to human capital, and thus to earning power; this was the assumption underlying the Mincer equation. The hypothesised link between added experience and additional earning power only seems to be borne out, however, by the experience of full-time employees in the UK. As we saw in Table 3, part-time experience seems to have a *negative* effect on pay, if anything.

The part-time pay gap for women in 1970 was of roughly the same order of magnitude as that for full-time women: now it is more than twice as large. After a sharp decline in the 1970s, the part-time pay gap rose in the 1980s (Harkness, 1996), and, though falling again, it remains substantial, as Figure 4 shows.

---

1 'Part-time', incidentally, is not a clear-cut category. The OECD regards people working fewer than 30 hours a week as part-time. The ASHE considers basic hours fewer than or equal to 30 to define part-time work – but 25 hours is the cut-off for teachers. Labour Force Survey (LFS) respondents define part-time for themselves – and the LFS part-timer definition excludes students.

Figure 4   **The part-time gender pay gap* in the UK**

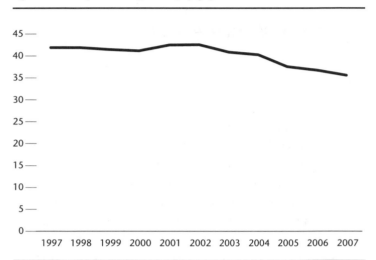

*Mean male full-time hourly earnings minus mean female part-time hourly earnings expressed as a percentage of mean male full-time hourly earnings. All figures excluding overtime.
Source: Office of National Statistics

The part-time pay penalty

This figure shows the gap in relation to full-time male employees, but it is also important to look at the relationship between the pay of full-time and part-time female employees – what has been termed the 'part-time pay penalty'. Women who work part time have hourly pay that is more than 20 per cent less than that of their full-time sisters.[2] As Manning and Petrongolo (2008) point

---

2   Interestingly, however, part-time women actually earn more on average than part-time men. And male part-timers also face a 'pay penalty' – actually slightly larger for men than for women. Male part-timers, a small minority of the part-time workforce, are mainly young (especially students) or drawn from the semi-retired; women part-timers, on the other hand, are drawn from across the age range.

out, however, this cannot be taken, as some seem to have done, as an indicator of the penalty incurred by a woman switching from full-time to part-time pay. Women who work part time have very different personal characteristics from those of full-time women, and they do very different jobs, as Table 5 shows.[3]

Table 5 **Distribution of women's employment between full-time and part-time work, 2000**

Ranked occupation	% of all full-time women	% of all part-time women
1 Teachers	8.7	4.5
2 Other professionals	5.2	1.7
3 Nurses	4.8	4.6
4 Other associate professionals	9.3	5.2
5 Corporate managers	13.1	3.4
6 Higher-skill services	3.2	1.6
7 Higher-level clerical	13.2	11.1
8 Other managers	3.5	0.9
9 Skilled trades	2.3	1.1
10 Lower-level clerical	14.2	12.6
11 Caring services	7.6	15.8
12 Other personal services	3.4	6.1
13 Sales assistants	3.6	14.7
14 Other low-skill occupations	6.9	7.6
15 Cleaners	1.0	9.1
	100	100

Source: Excerpted from Connolly and Gregory (2008)

3   The occupational classifications in Table 5 are ranked by qualifications required.

Manning and Petrongolo (2008: F30) spell out the differences between full-time and part-time female employees:

> Women working PT are more likely than FT women to be less-educated, older, white, in a couple with dependent children who are both numerous and young, to be working in small establishments, in shops, hotels and restaurants, in a temporary job, with low job tenure and in low-level occupations. 28% of FT women are in professional or managerial occupations compared to 11% of PT women while 52% of PT women are in personal service, sales or elementary occupations compared to 24% of FT women. Almost one in four PT women work as a care assistant, a shop assistant or a cleaner.

When these differences are controlled for, the authors point out, the part-time penalty shrinks to around 3 per cent (ibid.: F47).

There has been particular concern about the way in which some women who switch from full-time to part-time employment on their return to work after childbirth suffer a decline in occupational status, and presumably pay. This has been called the 'hidden brain drain' and seen as a waste of women's skills. Connolly and Gregory (2008: F53) claim that 'at the very least 14% and probably nearer one-quarter of women switching from full to part-time work move to an occupation at a lower level of qualification'. Rather confusingly, however, there are significant numbers of women who upgrade as they switch from full-time to part-time work, taking jobs that could be associated with upward career progression. In one survey 17 per cent of those switching from full-time to part-time work went up in occupational status.

Connolly and Gregory draw particular attention to the way in which women managers switch to lower-status jobs on becoming part time:

> Downgrading affects as many as 29% of women from professional and corporate management jobs … the most frequent 'victims' of downgrading, willing or otherwise, are women in smaller-scale managerial positions, in restaurants, salons and shops, almost half of whom shed their managerial and supervisory responsibilities and revert to being standard personal service or sales assistants. (Ibid.: F72)

But is it legitimate to call these women 'victims', even if the word is in inverted commas? Switching to part-time employment can be, as Paull (2008: F8) has noted, an optimal response to the constraints faced by women when children or other caring responsibilities limit the time available for paid work. Part-time arrangements are usually flexible and allow women to re-enter work on their own terms. And it's surely likely that some at least of the observed 'downgrading' of women's occupations after return to work is deliberately chosen. Given their new families, women may deliberately choose to return to jobs that carry less responsibility and less stress. They may accept a trade-off of lower status and pay in return for more convenient working hours, the opportunity to work at home, or shorter travel. To the extent that this is true, occupational downgrading is not a 'loss' to the woman. If they were to be obliged to return to their old job, even on a part-time basis, they might in some sense be worse off. To support this view, there is strong evidence provided by Booth and van Ours (2008), among others, that women in part-time employment are happier at work than men and – perhaps more tellingly – happier than women who work full time.

Interestingly, as with many *parti pris* authors in this field, Booth and van Ours find it odd that women enjoy part-time work, suggesting that they 'are conditioned to like being at home ... if ... society makes it hard for them to combine work and family, by providing little or inappropriate child care or by institutionalising low female pay, then it is hardly surprising that women will want to work fewer hours in the market sector' (ibid.: F95).

These authors appear to resist the view that women whose choices they disagree with are autonomous actors and seem to regard them as having very little choice in their behaviour and patterns of employment. There are certainly many women whose options are tightly constrained by family background, their own upbringing and educational choices, but this seems to take an unnecessarily pessimistic view of the options for the majority of women currently working part time.

7 POLICIES

Bearing in mind what is known about the nature and causes of the UK's gender pay gap, what policies have been proposed to reduce it – and how effective are they likely to be?

Pay audits, equal value and comparable worth

UK equal pay legislation is not simply concerned with trying to ensure that men and women are paid the same for identical jobs. As we have seen, since 1983 it has been recognised that men and women often do very different jobs, and so the legislation also applies to work 'of equal value', or the closely related 'comparable worth', the concept more commonly known in North America.[1]

In recent years, the emphasis on work of equal value has increased. The public sector has been required to conduct pay audits to check whether men and women doing jobs of equal value are treated equally. The two most important actions to which this has led are the 'Agenda for Change' in the National Health Service and the Single Status Agreement for local authorities. In these areas, job evaluation schemes have featured strongly.

---

1   In the 1980s, comparable worth was a big issue in the USA. President Reagan, who opposed the concept, memorably called it a 'cockamamie idea'. Some wide-reaching applications of the principle were eventually defeated in the courts, but interest has revived recently with Hillary Clinton and Barack Obama both having advocated new legislation.

Job evaluation schemes attempt to classify jobs in an organisation into a hierarchy, often on a points basis, with higher points being associated with positions on a new consolidated pay scale. One well-known approach, first developed 60 years ago, is the Hay system, a brand owned by the Hay Group. This is an analytical scheme, which case law shows to provide some defence against equal pay claims in front of employment tribunals. A group of Hay analysts, working from job descriptions and other information, produce a profile under three main headings – 'know-how', problem-solving and accountability. Know-how embraces knowledge, skill and experience (human capital, in economists' language); problem-solving involves the complexity of thinking and analysis required; while accountability looks at the responsibility of the post and its degree of autonomy in decision-making. Each element is broken down further into various levels.

In a curious way this schematic approach rather echoes the nineteenth-century labour theory of value, the intellectual inspiration of Marxism and the basis for pay structures in the Soviet bloc. The idea that there is something intrinsic about the work process that should determine pay is deeply rooted; this type of analysis allows little influence for market forces, nor for individuals' performance: it is all about the characteristics of the job, which is reduced to a series of discrete elements, each of which can be given a points score.

If these evaluation schemes are to bite at all and justify their use, they are expected to throw up anomalies in existing pay schemes. Given that the point of the exercise is to improve women's pay, it is not surprising that they do so. The corollary is that the pay of men may often have to be reduced. This predictably causes considerable unhappiness and conflict. Evaluation schemes carried out by local authorities under the Single Status Agreement have produced examples of major cuts in pay for some council workers (mainly male but including some females), many of whom were not particularly highly paid in the first place.[2]

And the knock-on consequences have been highly problematic. Unions have tried to broker deals to 'red-circle' existing salaries for men whose salaries are due to be cut, protecting their pay for a limited period. This of course adds to the cost of the job evaluation exercise, which the European Court of Justice has also inflated by the requirement to backdate higher pay for women for six years.

Faced with huge bills – central government has offered little in the way of extra financial help – local authorities are threatened with having to make job cuts. Unions have attempted to head this off by making deals to phase in new pay schemes gradually. But no-win, no-fee lawyers have moved in to take up the case of women whose potential pay gains have been reduced by union agreements; unions have been embarrassed to find themselves on the receiving end of discrimination and equal pay cases in front of employment tribunals.[3] This is one of the reasons for the huge increase in tribunal claims in relation to equal pay, from 8,229 in 2004/05 to 44,013 in 2006/07, which we noted earlier. These cases also generate very complicated judgements, which often go

---

2   In Burnley, Lancashire, some staff have faced pay cuts of £5,000. In early 2008, 25 per cent of Staffordshire County Council staff were scheduled to receive a pay cut (as against 45 per cent gaining). Similarly in Birmingham 3,000 council workers out of 19,000 were to suffer a reduction in pay.

3   In June 2006, women members of the GMB won a case against their union for indirect discrimination by protecting men's pay during Single Status negotiations; ironically the GMB organiser was herself a woman. The verdict was, however, overturned on appeal.

to appeal: in 2006/07, 37 per cent of Employment Appeal Tribunal cases concerned public sector issues.

Even when the dust settles on exercises of this kind, there are likely to be longer-term problems. For the pay levels determined by job evaluation are unlikely to be market-clearing. If the pay of council office cleaners or care workers (mainly female) is raised in relation to people working with bins or safety inspectors (mainly male), a likely outcome is that more women will seek office cleaning or care jobs[4] than there are posts available, while there will be a shortage of people willing to work on bins or inspecting premises. Experience suggests that organisations will then try to get round the pay structure with devices such as 'market supplements' or 'golden hellos' for workers in short supply. This may then undermine the pay equality that was the purpose of the whole costly exercise. And employers may try to cut the number of jobs in fields where it has become more expensive to hire workers: women may find job opportunities with councils drying up and end up taking lower-paid jobs in the private sector. So the longer-term consequences of pay evaluation schemes for gender pay equality are ambiguous. As in so many cases, apparently laudable ideas to 'improve' the workings of the market lead to consequences that are not fully anticipated by their proponents.

Despite the problems associated with the application of equal pay for work of equal value in the public sector, many union leaders and politicians are pressing for pay audits and job evaluations in the private sector. Derek Simpson of Amicus said in 2006: 'the pay gap between men and women is due to

---

4   Paradoxically, by making traditionally 'female' jobs more attractive, evaluation schemes may tend to reinforce, rather than diminish, any gender segregation in the labour market.

discrimination by employers not because women make bad career choices ... without compulsory pay audits, women will wait till doomsday for equal pay'. The TUC has said: 'Mandatory equal pay audits would help increase transparency in pay systems in the private sector where the pay gap remains high.' Susan Anderson of the CBI, however, has argued that such audits are 'cumbersome, labour- and resource-intensive and do not address the underlying causes of the gap'. The Women and Work Commission, therefore, shied away from recommending compulsion. So has the government: its proposed package of measures to promote gender equality, launched in June 2008, avoided audits for the private sector.

But what might happen if mandatory audits *were* introduced? Canada has some experience of this. Ontario introduced the most comprehensive comparable-worth policy in North America in 1987 with its Pay Equity Act. This applied not only to the public sector but also to private sector firms with more than ten employees.

The legislation was proactive. Rather than female employees having to make a case that they were underpaid, employers in firms with more than a hundred employees were required to publish a pay-equity plan identifying predominantly male and predominantly female jobs within the firm, to undertake job evaluations on the basis of skill, effort, responsibility and working conditions, and to pay the first instalments of any consequent awards according to a fairly tight timetable.

At first, male/female job comparisons were to be made within establishments, comparing job with job. Later, however, the Act was amended to admit other comparisons, in particular the proxy method of locating comparators outside the immediate organisation, for example using Mincer-style regressions linking men's earnings to job characteristics to predict what women's pay 'should' be.[5]

The evidence[6] indicates that the Ontario law did not succeed in reducing the gender pay gap. There was a lack of compliance among smaller firms, deadlines were missed by larger firms (particularly since unions seem to have dragged their heels in approving schemes), there turned out to be relatively little 'under-valued' female work in large firms, and there was a general lack of male comparators for female jobs. Of course, the legislation held only *within* firms, so low-paying firms continued to be low-paying firms even where there had been some reduction in internal pay inequality. And firms with a predominantly male workforce could continue to increase pay. There was some evidence that employment growth was slower for females in male-dominated jobs and for males in 'female' jobs.

In addition, firms found the pay equity process to be an administrative burden, resulting in significant indirect costs. There were no measurable offsetting effects on productivity and morale. Any advantage to women in traditionally female occupations was partly offset by disadvantages to the minority of women in traditionally 'male' occupations where pay was held to be too high.

The suggested solution to the lack of success of the legislation in narrowing the pay gap involved centralising wage determination, or imposing external evaluations on firms. The Ontario government backed off, however, and recommended switching instead to a complaints-based system.

---

5   Such regressions have also been used in court cases in the USA alleging discrimination under Title VII of the Civil Rights Act 1964. The difficulties of using them in evidence are discussed by Epstein (1992: 375–85).

6   See, for instance, Baker and Fortin (2004).

Government procurement policies

It has been suggested by the TUC and by the Women and Work Commission that government procurement policies could be used as another means to promote pay equality. They see '... procurement as a significant opportunity to spread good practice on the range of equal opportunities ... Business stakeholders suggested to us that procurement could be a more effective incentive than regulation to change behaviour' (Women and Work Commission, 2006: 93).

Government procurement from the private sector predates the modern state, going back hundreds of years. Its significance was increased in the 1980s and 1990s by the development of contracting out of public services during the Thatcher and Major administrations. This was part of the Conservatives' attempt to break up public sector monopolies and the power of public sector unions, but the principle was continued by New Labour. Although it has had some impact in reducing costs, contracting out has been increasingly hedged around with requirements not to pay less than existing rates of pay, and any workers in danger of being disadvantaged by transfers of managerial responsibility are now substantially protected by both British and European law.

The introduction of the optimistically named 'best value' regime for procurement in 1997 paradoxically allowed public authorities to take a wider definition of the criteria for a successful tender. As a consequence a growing number of social criteria can be incorporated into procurement policies of central government and local authorities.[7] The Office of Government Commerce has

---

7   Now worth about £125 billion, according to the House of Commons Business, Enterprise and Regulatory Reform Committee (2008: 32).

issued guidance on this. The guidance[8] states that social issues can be incorporated into procurement 'where they are relevant and proportionate to the subject matter of the contract', although it points out that 'they need to be addressed in a way that is consistent with value for money policy, the UK procurement regulations and the EU Treaty principles and procurement directives'.

Although gender pay equality could be emphasised more strongly, a generalised commitment to equality is already common in procurement offers.[9] It has to jostle for attention, however, with a large number of other important social issues, including community employment creation, environmental sustainability, innovation, fair trade, 'building good relations' with trade unions, and the development of workforce skills – all of which are frequently incorporated into the criteria that contractors must meet. How far these factors are important in practice in determining bid outcomes is unclear.

A number of things *are* clear, however: one is that many of these criteria are producer-driven rather than consumer-focused, and the interests of the taxpayer (the original justification for contracting out) are downplayed. Another is that compliance with a wide range of non-technical criteria adds considerably to the burdens of those submitting tenders, as those with experience of this will testify. A third observation, partly a consequence of this, is that these additional criteria are likely to deter smaller, start-up firms that have less experience of form-filling and are less likely to have developed policies relating to a full

---

8   www.ogc.gov.uk/documents/Social_Issues.pdf.
9   The GLA and the Olympic Delivery Authority explicitly incorporate equality requirements, for example.

range of social issues.[10] It is perhaps not surprising that some 'business stakeholders' – presumably those larger, more established enterprises with experience of these matters – advised the Women and Work Commission to promote pay equality in this manner: by doing so, they would reduce the number of potential competitors.

It's also worth pointing out that many of the areas for which the biggest public sector contracts are placed (for example, construction and road and railway maintenance) employ relatively few women, and thus even the most determined application[11] of equal pay principles within those areas would have little direct impact on the aggregate pay gap.

Gender quotas for top jobs

Many politicians have expressed concern at the dearth of women in the most high-paying jobs. Table 6 shows that women remain a small minority on the boards of top companies in the UK (although the proportion is higher than the EU average). There has been a growth in the number of female non-executive directors, but they still constitute only 14.5 per cent of all non-executives. The number of female executive directors has barely grown since 2000 and stands at 3.6 per cent of the total. At the time of writing there are just two CEOs in the FTSE 100. Around a quarter of these top companies have no female directors at all.

---

10 An OFT report in 2003 drew attention to the way in which small businesses were deterred from bidding for public sector contracts because of the bureaucracy involved. Note also that women are over-represented among employees in small businesses.

11 And it would have to be determined. Many government contracts often involve subcontracting, which would need to be policed as well.

Table 6 **Female directors in FTSE 100 companies**

	2000	2001	2002	2003	2004	2005	2006	2007
Female executive directorships	11 2.0%	10	15	17	17	14	15	13 3.6%
Female non-executive directorships	60 9.1%	65	69	84	93	107	102	110 14.5%
Companies with no female directors	42	43	39	32	31	22	23	24

Note: There are more female directorships than female directors as some individuals hold more than one directorship
Source: Sealy et al. (2007)

This is one of the most obvious manifestations of the 'glass ceiling' that is often assumed to limit women's full participation in the economy. Should something be done about it? In Norway, since 1 January 2008 it has been compulsory for companies to have 40 per cent[12] female board members. The Norwegian legislation, foreshadowed by the introduction of a voluntary scheme for companies five years earlier,[13] has succeeded in raising the number of women on boards dramatically. Within a few days of the law taking effect, virtually every single publicly listed company had a woman on its board and the proportion of females on boards was close to 38 per cent (Holmes, 2008).

Are there lessons for the UK? One point to make is that the legislation evolved in the context of a political system that has had quotas of female candidates for more than thirty years, an

12 Small boards are not required to have this precise minimum.
13 The law was applied to state-owned companies in 2004.

experience that is not mirrored here. It has more political support than such a measure could initially count on in the UK. It has not, however, received total support in Norway, with the country's Confederation of Enterprise being opposed. Many smaller companies are avoiding stock market listing to evade the new legislation, a reminder that similar legislation in the UK could be a further spur to the trend for companies to delist and go private – or transfer to other national jurisdictions where the quotas did not apply.

Who are the new female directors in Norway? It appears that the expansion has largely been in non-executives: there remain very few women in top executive positions. The new board members have been women disproportionately recruited from politics and the civil service, with the best-qualified women, graduates of the country's leading educational establishments, often holding multiple directorships. Such a pattern would probably be repeated in the UK, were similar legislation to be introduced.

There is no tradition of gender quotas and positive discrimination in the UK, and the introduction of Norwegian-style legislation would be a dramatic change in philosophy. It could contravene European law – Norway is of course not a member of the EU – so it probably could not be introduced by the UK in isolation.[14] Even if it were allowed, in the UK context of significant minority ethnic groups with their own equality concerns, it is likely that quotas for women would lead to a demand for ethnic quotas.[15] Whether this is a road down which any political party would wish to go seems doubtful.

---

14 Germany and the Netherlands, however, have announced their intention to move in the same direction.
15 The same would go, for example, for people with disabilities. Interestingly, disability quotas were briefly tried in the UK but abandoned.

If gender quotas for company boards were nevertheless brought in, would they in any case make a significant difference to the gender pay gap? Their impact on the aggregate pay gap would surely be minimal, given the small numbers of places on company boards in relation to the total population. But even within the population of top company posts they would be unlikely to have much of an impact. It is known that the mean gender pay gap among company directors is quite high – the Institute of Directors Rewards Survey put it at 22 per cent in 2007.[16] Were gender quotas to be introduced, the majority of new women directors would be non-executives who typically earn relatively small amounts (a quarter are unpaid) and are usually part time. A case can certainly be made for the symbolic importance of getting more women into these prominent positions, but it is entirely possible that a big influx of female non-executive directors could actually widen the gender pay gap on company boards by dragging down the average earnings of female directors – another example of the inappropriateness of focusing exclusively on the pay gap as an indicator of gender equality.

Childcare

Another frequently touted policy is the expansion of nursery and other childcare provision, and their subsidy by the government. A common view is that childcare provision in the UK is inadequate and too expensive. In this country parents pay about 70 per cent of the cost of childcare by comparison with the European average of 30 per cent (Hakim et al., 2008). Reducing the real cost of quality

---

16 http://press.iod.com/newsdetails.aspx?ref=308&m=2&mi-62&ms=&print=true.

childcare to parents is seen as one way of strengthening women's commitment to the workforce and thus indirectly reducing the gender pay gap (Plantenga and Remery, 2006; Gregory and Connolly, 2008; Booth and van Ours, 2008).

Is there some sort of market failure in childcare provision? It is not entirely clear. It can be argued that there are externalities in the provision of quality childcare – we all benefit if children grow up happy and secure and, in relation to the theme of this paper, this provision enables women to return to the workforce earlier and for more hours than would otherwise be the case.[17] Arguments about externalities are, however, rarely quantified. Is there a shortage of supply? In some areas of the country there may be shortages of nursery places, but in others there seems if anything to be an excess supply (Hakim et al., 2008: 33).

One issue is that the government has taken an increasingly strong regulatory position in relation to childcare, with an emphasis on bringing childcare out of the home, on increasing the ratio of carers to children, on laying down formal curricula for pre-school education, on insisting on qualifications and criminal records checks for carers and those employed in nurseries, and Ofsted inspections and documentation. One result of this is the decline of the childminder: the numbers of registered childminders fell from 98,500 in 1997 to 68,348 a decade later (although there may be a suspicion that increased regulation has led to an increase in unofficial childminding, probably not a good outcome). Another result is a substantial increase in

---

17 It has also been argued that there might be a market failure if women who had children were unaware in advance of the cost of childcare. This seems not to credit women with very much sense, and such alleged ignorance could be used to justify subsidies to virtually any economic activity on the grounds of incomplete information.

costs for private sector nurseries, which has led to higher fees for parents.

In some sense, perhaps, there has also been a 'crowding out' of private provision of childcare by the expansion of public sector provision. Since 1998, the Sure Start initiative has developed from beginnings in coordinating family support to a current concern with providing centre-based daycare. The National Audit Office has expressed concern about whether the funding for this partial nationalisation of childcare is sustainable, but meanwhile it is arguably undermining parts of the market for private childcare.

The second leg of the government's childcare policy is the Early Years Entitlement, which is a payment to nurseries to provide three- and four-year-olds with twelve and a half hours of pre-school activity for 33 weeks a year.[18] Parents are also entitled to Working Tax Credits linked to formal childcare, though the take-up is not huge, particularly among single parents.

Evidence suggests that parents prefer good informal childcare (including family and friends) to formal nurseries or daycare centres, and they prefer private nurseries to public sector provision, though the funding mechanisms are biased in the opposite directions. The think tank Policy Exchange (ibid.) makes plausible recommendations about switching funding to support informal childcare and even subsidising mothers to stay at home, but clearly this is part of a wider agenda and is not concerned with the impact of childcare arrangements on the gender pay gap.

Certainly some forms of childcare support can have an impact

---

18   This provision, though no doubt welcome to many parents, clearly could not provide the basis for a parent to return to a full-time or even a significant part-time job. The financial resources used to support this could be better deployed in other directions if the main purpose was to encourage parents back into work earlier.

on encouraging women to return to work. Even though the effect was modest, the Institute for Fiscal Studies (2006) found that the childcare element of tax credits did induce some single parents to return to work earlier and this may have helped them to higher levels of pay over time. This, however, is only part of the rationale for stronger taxpayer support of childcare.

If the UK emulated Scandinavia, where around 1.5 per cent of GDP goes on government spending to support pre-school childcare, would it be likely to have much impact on the gender pay gap? Bear in mind that there would be a very substantial 'deadweight loss': that is, if childcare subsidies were available to all, the main beneficiaries would be women in work who already make their own childcare arrangements.[19] If, on the other hand, it was means tested, experience suggests that the take-up would be relatively low.

Sweden, which is often held up as an example of good practice in publicly subsidised childcare, provides a cautionary tale. Despite the high levels of government spending Sweden has put into childcare for many years, its gender pay gap remains above the EU average. Women who work are crowded into the public sector (only 25 per cent of Swedish female employees work in the private sector), and only 1.5 per cent of Swedish senior management are women, less than in the UK.[20] So, although there may be other reasons for increasing state support for pre-schoolers, such as social inclusion, it seems unlikely that even quite massive UK investment in childcare would do much to shift the gender pay gap.

---

19 According to Policy Exchange, formal childcare of the kind supported by public subsidy 'is most commonly used by highly educated and higher-earning parents' (Hakim et al. 2008: 47).

20 Catherine Hakim, quoted in Moorhead (2004).

Education

Part of the explanation for women earning less is that, despite girls now significantly outperforming boys at school, and young women doing better than men at university, female educational and training choices lead them into lower-paid occupations and jobs.

This is an issue that concerned the Women and Work Commission. In their analysis they emphasised that gender stereotypes persist and that these begin in primary school. Teachers do not do enough to combat this, it is argued. And, as a result of government attempts to boost exam results, girls are allowed to opt out of science and mathematics too early. Careers advisers do not make girls sufficiently aware of differences in pay rates between jobs, and they are not given enough opportunities for work experience in jobs where women have historically been under-represented. They recommend that more be done by government and schools to promote entry into jobs that offer women higher pay and career progression.

This is unexceptionable. However, there often seems almost to be an assumption that girls and young women are ignorant or irrational (while presumably boys and men are better informed), but this does not seem plausible today. Structural barriers to entry into male-dominated, higher-paying employment are far less than in the past, and most leading professions have active groups proselytising for more female entrants. Schemes to encourage a wider choice of occupations by young people – women into carpentry, men into childcare – are worthy and interesting, and may persuade some youngsters to try something different. It is possible that the planned move away from A-levels to a wider system of diplomas, or even a continental European Baccalaureatestyle school qualification, would delay subject choice and lead to women studying a different mix of subjects at university. Placing too much faith on this is risky, however, as the picture of female employment concentrated in a limited range of occupations is consistent across Europe (Eurostat, 2008).

Even where women study a potentially high-earning subject at college, however – economics or sciences, say – they are less likely than men to go into the higher-earning jobs to which these qualifications give access. For instance, while many young men with economics degrees go into the City, similarly qualified young women are more likely to pursue jobs in teaching, academic research or the civil service. Commentators such as Catherine Hakim would, as we have seen, argue that these preferences are deeply rooted and not easily affected by government initiatives.

Strengthening the right to request flexible working

If more women switching from full time to part time work on re-entering the workforce were able to continue in their existing jobs, the loss of pay and career prospects associated with occupational downgrading, discussed earlier, would be reduced. Women who continued longer in senior roles would be more likely to keep pace with men, and the widening of the gender pay gap associated with age would be less marked.

In fact, the position is not as bad as it is sometimes painted. In 2005, the Labour Force Survey showed that 28.5 per cent of full-time women employees, and 27.3 per cent of part-timers, had flexible conditions of one sort or another. And a high proportion of women who remain with their existing employer are able to stay in the same occupation even if they want to reduce hours. Campaigners would like to increase the numbers doing this. Currently over 3.5 million women with a child under six or a disabled child under eighteen are entitled to request flexible working, and the government is planning to extend this right to all those with children aged up to seventeen. Although a large majority of formal requests for flexibility under existing legislation are met, this may not be the case in future if the right is extended. And even now, of those employers prepared to accept flexible working by a returner, 'only two-thirds would allow her to remain at the same level of seniority', it is claimed (Reeves, 2008). Many lobbyists would therefore like to narrow the grounds on which an employer can refuse such a request,[21] perhaps shifting the burden of proof, as in the Netherlands, to make employers provide a convincing case that there would be damage to the firm from, say, a job-sharing arrangement for senior managers, who are the most likely to have such requests refused.

Women who stay with their existing employers on return to work are one issue. A bigger problem arguably arises when a woman has left her previous employer, tries to find a new part-time job on re-entry to the labour market, and finds that advertised posts are rarely offered on a part-time basis in higher occupational categories. So it is argued that employers should be induced to offer a wider range of part-time jobs, at the same rate of pay, pro rata, as full-time jobs.

Businesses are 'mostly resistant to creating senior level part-time jobs' (Women and Work Commission, 2006: 34); they need to 'improve the quality of part-time jobs' (Manning and

---

21 The current grounds for refusal under the Employment Rights Act 1996 are: burden of additional costs; detrimental effect on ability to meet consumer demand; inability to reorganise work among existing staff; detrimental impact on quality; detrimental impact on performance; insufficiency of work during the periods the employee proposes to work; and planned structural changes.

Petrongolo, 2008). It is apparently only excessive caution and inertia which stops them doing so (House of Commons Trade and Industry Committee, 2005).

But is it quite that simple? Examples of successful part-time work in higher occupational categories quoted, for example, by the Women and Work Commission tend to be from the fields of teaching, higher education, nursing, and local government and the civil service. In these areas there tend to be discrete tasks, which are fairly routine and involve little decision-making responsibility (teaching a particular university module, caring for a particular group of patients for a particular period of time, assessing applications for planning permission or evaluating policy proposals). Many analysts, themselves usually academics or from a public sector or union background, possibly generalise too easily from these examples.

Businesses at the tough end argue that part-time employment is much easier to implement in some jobs than in others. In managerial roles, in particular, there can be real problems. There is a range of preferred arrangements to match up, with some people wanting to work two or three days a week, some wanting to work only during the school year, or during hours when children are normally at school or nursery. The cost and effort of finding acceptable matches – a person wanting to work Monday and Tuesday, with another willing to work Wednesday to Friday – can be considerable. In such a case there are two lots of hiring costs, two lots of induction, two lots of payroll documentation, coordination time for the managers, the danger of delays, and of subordinates playing one manager off against another; problems of covering for holidays, problems associated with turnover (where the firm has to find another difficult match when one part-time manager leaves), and difficulties when part-time managers want to change their hours of work.

There is the further issue that many managerial roles cannot easily be timetabled into a standard working day: work may have to be taken home, or during periods of high activity longer hours may have to be worked to ensure a project or a special order is brought in on time. Part-time managers may be unwilling or unable to handle issues like this.

Larger firms in routinised fields may find it possible to adjust to flexible working without excessive cost, but smaller firms in dynamic markets with heterogeneous products or projects may find it prohibitively costly: small and medium enterprises frequently complain that they bear a disproportionate burden when labour market regulation is increased. Furthermore, some of the burden may fall on fellow workers. A recent survey by the Engineering Employers Federation, while documenting such benefits of flexible working as improved motivation and reduced turnover, also showed that employers believe it creates problems by putting extra pressure on other employees who have to adjust their routines to accommodate those working 'flexibly'.[22]

In July 2008 employers' opposition to proposals to extend flexible working and maternity leave received support from an unexpected quarter. Nicola Brewer, chief executive of the Equality and Human Rights Commission, expressed fear that extensions of these rights could have a damaging effect. Ms Brewer was quoted as saying that 'the thing I worry about is that the current legislation and regulations have had the unintended consequences of making women a less attractive prospect to employers'.[23]

22 *Financial Times*, 5 May 2008.
23 *The Times*, 14 July 2008.

8 SO SHOULD WE *REALLY* MIND THE GAP?

Let us now review the position. We have established that there is a significant differential between the hourly pay of men and women employed full time: this is the headline gender pay gap. The gap has, however, diminished over time – and this trend is very likely to continue, though there may be blips from time to time. Younger women are much more highly educated than their predecessors. They are having children later, and returning to employment more rapidly (Simon and Whiting, 2007). They are diversifying their employment between occupations. The economy is becoming increasingly 'weightless', with services of all kinds increasing as a share of employment, and manufacturing and primary production falling: this trend favours those sectors where women are concentrated. All of these factors are likely to reduce the gender pay gap over time; some analysts even predict it will go into reverse in due course.

This process will, however, take time, and it is argued that the pace is too slow. But can it easily be accelerated?

Despite claims to the contrary, there isn't a great deal of evidence that the pay gap is caused by employer discrimination. One reason why it may be difficult to prove discrimination, as Epstein (1992: 381) argues, is that it may not be present. Rather, part of the pay gap may be accounted for by compensating pay differentials and much of the rest results from choices made by women and men in relation to their education and training, their occupation and employer, their work–life balance and decisions to have families, as well as their attitudes to and expectations of work.

These factors are difficult to influence, at least in the short run. We have seen that there are doubts about the effectiveness of the policies currently proposed. In some cases these policies may be counterproductive, or lead to undesirable side effects. Insofar as they attempt to make fundamental changes in values and attitudes, especially those relating to family life and the care and education of children, they involve trying to influence the most intimate choices of individuals. Some may see this as intrusive and unnecessary. Others may just see the task as hugely overambitious. Should government really assume responsibility for altering the behaviour of hundreds of thousands of employers, and the individual, personal choices of millions of women and men?

Misleading economics

Some of the arguments put forward for government intervention are spurious, and naively – or perhaps deliberately – misrepresent how economies work and how pay is determined. Take, for instance, the claim, reported earlier, that women are 'cheated' of £330,000 over their lifetime because of the pay gap.[1] This back-of-the-envelope calculation represents the difference in average earnings of men and women over a working life. We can ask a 'what if?' question: what if a magic wand was waved to erase the pay gap and raise all women's pay to that of their male counterparts? What would happen?

---

1   Perhaps an example of what David Henderson has called 'do-it-yourself economics' (Henderson, 1986).

Most obviously, completely equal pay would not be a sustainable equilibrium. Women's jobs would be likely to be lost on a large scale in the private sector, as no government power can force profit-seeking enterprises to continue to hire as many people at a markedly higher wage. Application of complete pay equality in the public sector would also have adverse tendencies: it would raise taxation, or create job losses, or both; the experience of the Single Status Agreement graphically demonstrates this.

As Reeves has argued, 'there are grave dangers in relying on economic arguments ... such estimates are difficult to generate and are open to subjective manipulation'.[2] For example, take the argument that skills are being wasted, and output would be increased by up to 2 per cent of GDP if women who leave the workforce or return to lower-paid jobs after childbirth instead returned to their previous full-time jobs. This does not bear close examination. An increase in the labour supply of this magnitude would almost certainly tend to bring earnings down; it might also lead to male workers and younger female workers being displaced from the workforce. Output would not rise by the amount assumed. Moreover, given that a large proportion of occupational downgrading and switching to part-time work is chosen by the women concerned, there would be a welfare loss to offset any output gain.[3]

---

2   Reeves (2008). He points out that 'another recent study even found that £5 billion is lost each year as a result of bosses' failure to say "thank you" to their staff'. This, he wryly remarks, suggests that there are easier ways to boost output than through trying to get more women into full-time work.

3   The limitations of gross domestic product as a measure of economic welfare are well known. Economics lecturers have long drawn their students' attention to the paradox that a woman who employs a gardener – like Jane Wyman in that wonderful film *All that Heaven Allows* – would reduce GDP should she marry him. No wonder her relationship with Rock Hudson was doomed.

More generally, critics of existing pay differentials sometimes seem not really to understand how economies work, and talk in reified abstractions:

> Women are more likely to work in lower-paying occupations, including the five 'c's: cleaning, catering, caring, cashiering and clerical work. These occupations are relatively low paid at least partly because *society does not appear to value the skills required in these occupations as much as it does others*. (Women and Work Commission, 2006: 55)

What does this mean, exactly? It is not a question of 'society' valuing anything. What we have here is a situation where there are large numbers of people – mainly but by no means exclusively women – who are able and willing to do these jobs, which require little formal training or experience. Other individuals – men and women – are prepared to pay a certain amount directly (cleaners and carers in particular are often employed by households) or indirectly (we buy products from firms that employ them) for their services. The interaction of supply and demand produce the pattern of pay we see, but this is nothing to do with how 'society' thinks. This is not Mrs Thatcher's often misunderstood observation that there is no such thing as society, but rather that there is no way in which a complex society can express a collective preference for the pattern of pay for millions of employees.

Too many politicians across the political spectrum claim the right – albeit with the best of intentions, no doubt – to make choices for us all. If they decree that lower-paid employees must be paid more, the likely consequence is that firms and individuals, who cannot be coerced into buying their services, will buy less of them. The consequence is that fewer people will be employed, and in the absence of other opportunities, unemployment will rise.

The Women and Work Commission and others make much of the view – and this is the whole 'comparable worth' argument – that jobs dominated (though not exclusively) by men, such as warehousing, transport driving and labouring, have similar skill levels to those used in 'the five "c"s'. The former jobs are, however, better paid.

Two comments can be made here. First, skills are not the only issue. These male-dominated jobs may have less attractive working conditions, so higher pay may be reflecting this. Second, employers will only pay higher wages in these jobs if they need to do so to attract enough applicants. Certainly private sector employers at least have no reason to pay more than they need to pay. If 'society' (again, read politicians) determines that drivers and labourers should be paid less, then the result is likely to be that some employees will leave, firms will experience a shortage of workers and output will fall.

Policy ineffectiveness and its consequences

We have seen that the policies proposed to narrow the pay gap may not have as significant an impact as their proponents claim. Governments are not all-powerful, though oddly people seem to think that in this area they can be.

Policies that are ineffective are nevertheless often costly to implement, involving both employers and government in significant expenditure of time and money. Firms, seeking to justify themselves, to politicians, interest groups and the media, are distracted from their core business into obsessive concern with workforce issues.

Unsuccessful policies produce frustration, anger and demands for further regulation. In this situation politicians rarely shrug their shoulders and give up. They try something else. The danger is that further, and potentially more damaging, labour market intervention then creeps up the political agenda. For many, the gender pay issue is part of a much wider critique of labour markets and this may lead to the kind of policies discussed in a paper prepared for the Equality Unit of the European Commission (Plantenga and Remery, 2006). Taking the point mentioned earlier, that more compressed wage structures are associated with smaller gender pay gaps, these authors touch on a number of policies that could be used to compress wages. These include a Europe-wide minimum wage, limits on executive pay and the reintroduction of centralised pay determination involving a stronger role for trade unions and other 'social partners'. In the UK such a fundamental shift in employment policy would constitute a return to the discredited labour market interventions of the past. A more compressed pay structure subject to regular government intervention and increased union power would run the risk of discouraging innovation and risk-taking, driving top earners abroad and reducing inward investment.

Even then, the pay gap might not behave in the way interventionists suppose. Remember that the headline gender pay gap is a statistical artefact which needs to be interpreted with care. Its size can change for reasons that are not obvious or fully understood – certainly not by those press commentators and pressure groups who regard this indicator as of such great importance. Women's labour force participation rate is a key element, and this can, as we have seen, be affected by changes in the birth rate, changes in the age of marriage or cohabitation and changes in the age gap between women and their partners. These factors could produce perverse changes in the pay gap. Moreover, if increased government intervention led to higher marginal tax rates, this could again alter behaviour in a way that is not entirely predictable.

Other pay and income gaps

The political and media emphasis on the gender pay gap should not cause us to forget that this statistic is only one of many pay gaps that it is possible to define. An obvious area to pursue is that of ethnic differentials. As we saw in Table 2, there is a significant gap in average pay between white workers and most ethnic minorities – although some minorities, Chinese and Indian, earn more on average than whites. Why should these gaps not be given more emphasis? All the same arguments apply.[4] In 2004 the Ethnic Minorities Task Force publicised pay differentials between black and white workers in exactly the same way as the gender pay gap: one report was headed 'Black pay gap robs minorities of £7,000 a year'.[5]

Having more than one pay gap as a target could, however, lead to problems. For policies can conflict. Suppose that an increase in the pay of Pakistanis, Bangladeshis and black workers relative to whites could be engineered in some way. This would, other things being equal, probably mean that the gender pay gap as officially measured would rise slightly – because the chief gainers in these minority groups would in the short run be male.[6]

---

4   Except that there is rather more evidence of direct discrimination against some ethnic minorities than there is against women. Yet despite this, in the UK as in most other countries, gender discrimination is seen as a more serious issue than ethnic or racial discrimination (OECD, 2008: ch. 3).

5   www.clickajob.co.uk/news-black-pay-gap.

6   A further complication is that it is increasingly obvious that some poor white

This is just one example of the way in which the gender pay gap interacts with other social concerns – something that has never been sufficiently emphasised in the policy debate. Take another example: an increase in female earnings associated with a reduction in the gender pay gap would have the effect of widening the disparity of income between households. This is because the UK has seen since the 1980s a dichotomy between 'work-rich' and 'work-poor' households (Simon and Whiting, 2007). There has been a growth of two-earner households, but also a growth of no-earner households (where there is a single workless parent or two partners, neither of whom works). Clearly an increase in female pay in a two-earner household increases the income gap between such households and work-poor households. So a decrease in one measure of inequality, the gender pay gap, increases another measure.

If this is true of society-wide measures of inequality, it is also the case that an increase in female earnings would primarily benefit white households, as ethnic minority women have lower participation rates (with some exceptions). Thus an increase in women's earnings would in the short run at least mean an increase in the income gap between white and minority ethnic households.

Disability is another area of concern. People with disabilities are far less likely to be top earners, and there is a substantial pay gap between the able and disabled sections of the population (Meager and Hill, 2005). Of those with disabilities, more men than

---

boys are performing very badly at school (worse than most ethnic minority groups) and face very poor job prospects, as Trevor Phillips of the Equality and Human Rights Commission has noted ('Poor white boys are victims too', *Sunday Times*, 27 April 2008).

women are in employment (Berthoud, 2006) and an increase in the pay of those with disabilities with respect to the able employed would probably have the incidental effect of marginally increasing the gender pay gap.

Religious belief is yet another area where there is claimed to be some degree of discrimination.[7] Although no estimates of a 'religious pay gap' have been published, it seems likely that some such gap exists. How does this relate to gender? It used to be assumed that women were more involved in religious activity, and thus this might be a further source of disadvantage. Loewenthal et al. (2002) have demonstrated, however, that this assumption was culture specific. Although Christian women are more religiously active than men, the reverse seems to be the case for Muslims, Jews and Hindus. It seems likely that Muslim men in particular may suffer some labour market disadvantage from their religion.

Finally, sexual orientation is another area that is protected by laws on discrimination. There is some evidence that gay men earn more than heterosexual men, a pay gap that is not thought to require redress. Why? It is not an entirely facetious question. If inequality is the issue – rather than poverty – why shouldn't we be concerned?

Drawing attention to these different sorts of pay gaps is not meant to trivialise any of these issues. But the point is that for too long there has been an emphasis on reducing the gender pay gap, rather than (say) redressing the low pay or poverty of more specific groups in the population – whether they comprise women or men. It is far from obvious that there is some sisterly mutuality of interest between Marjorie Scardino, Pearson's chief executive,

---

7   Weller et al.(2001).

The 'gay pay gap'

There is an interesting story around the gay pay gap. In a recent paper, Arabsheibani, Marin and Wadsworth (2005) use decomposition analysis of the kind discussed earlier to examine pay differences associated with sexual orientation. They observe that both gay men and lesbians earn more on average than their heterosexual counterparts. Yet their analysis indicates that gay men, while earning more than heterosexual men, show lower returns on their observable economic characteristics. It is possible, therefore, that there is some discrimination against them – though, as we have seen, other explanations may be plausible. Yet lesbian women, also earning more than heterosexual women, seem to get higher returns on their economic characteristics – which might suggest that there is discrimination *in their favour*.

It is not possible to form a definitive view on the basis of this one piece of work, but it illustrates once again that a raw pay gap between two groups of workers is an ambiguous piece of evidence when it comes to determining causation and thus shaping appropriate public policy. It also reminds us that a simple dichotomy between 'women' and 'men' is very misleading in a society where lifestyles vary considerably within, as well as between, genders.

and a £6-an-hour female cleaner, such that it transcends all other issues of inequality in the UK labour market.

Six impossible things before breakfast

Lewis Carroll's White Queen, in *Through the Looking Glass*, shocked Alice by declaring that she had often believed 'as many as six impossible things before breakfast'. Believing that the gender pay gap can ever be completely eliminated probably requires considerably more than six impossible things. It is rather more likely that a reverse gender pay gap – women earning more than men on average – might eventually emerge.[8]

For what would you need to close the gender pay gap completely? Men and women would need to have the same qualifications, in the same subjects, be employed in the same types of occupations in the same type of firms, have the same preferences between paid work and home work, share domestic tasks equally and take the same amount of time out of the workforce, have the same career plans and expectations, value the same attributes of jobs, take the same amount of time travelling to work and so on. Is this likely ever to be achieved? And would it be desirable?

I am not the first economist to admire Kurt Vonnegut's dystopian fable 'Harrison Bergeron'.[9] In this short story, total equality has been achieved by physically handicapping the most intelligent and talented members of society to bring them all down to the same level of ability and attainment, a process that is overseen by the United States Handicapper-General. Harrison Bergeron, the central character of the story, has exceptional intelligence, height, strength and good looks, and as a result he has to carry enormous

---

8 'A reverse gender pay gap should no longer be unthinkable' (Gregory and Connolly, 2008). It is interesting to speculate what might happen were women on average to start earning more than men – as we have seen, in some subgroups of the population they already do. Would this be considered a matter for public concern?

9 Published in his *Welcome to the Monkey House*.

handicaps. These include earphones that produce continuous distracting noises, three hundred pounds of excess weight, spectacles to give him headaches and cosmetic changes to make him ugly. Even then he can't be held back and stages a revolt on national television. Ultimately the only way he can be restrained is to shoot him.

In conclusion

Much writing and public comment on the gender pay gap starts from the premise that its existence is evidence of a strong and systematic bias against women in the labour market, that employers are in large measure to blame for this, and stronger government action is necessary to redress the balance. This paper has argued that this largely uncontested view is open to serious challenge.

There is most certainly a gender pay gap; but it has fallen, is likely to fall further and could even go into reverse. The full-time pay gap is a misleading and partial indicator of the economic status of women, and it does not indicate much about any real loss to the economy. Employer discrimination is not a major factor: the size of the pay gap depends on a range of factors, many of which are probably beyond the influence of government as they depend on the values, preferences and choices of individual men and women.

The size of the gap can fluctuate for obscure reasons, and its size relative to that of other countries means very little in isolation. Policies advocated to reduce the size of pay gap often show a misunderstanding of basic economics. They are unlikely to succeed but could create significant collateral damage. Their failure is likely to spread disillusion, which could lead to further government intervention with much more damaging consequences.

The gender pay gap is, furthermore, only one measure of inequality in a society and there is no obvious reason to privilege it over other concerns which may be of more importance. There are likely to be conflicts between policies to reduce the gender pay gap and those aimed at other types of disadvantage: this is rarely acknowledged.

Men and women are groups that are far too large and heterogeneous to benefit from sensible policy interventions going beyond the basic principle of equality of opportunity, already enshrined in law and increasingly embedded in practice in this country. Complete equality of outcome between men and women's pay is impossible to achieve in a free society of any complexity. All of this suggests that we should make far less of a song and dance about the gender pay gap.

REFERENCES

Arabsheibani, G. R., A. Marin and J. Wadsworth (2005), 'Gay pay in the UK', *Economica*, 72: 333–47.

Arrow, K. J. (1972), 'Models of job discrimination', in A. H. Pascal (ed.), *Racial Discrimination in Economic Life*, Lexington, MA: D. C. Heath.

Baker, M. and N. M. Fortin (2004), 'Comparable worth in a decentralised labour market: the case of Ontario', *Canadian Journal of Economics*, 37(4): 850–78.

Balcock, L. and S. Laschever (2003), *Women Don't Ask: Negotiation and the Gender Divide*, Princeton, NJ: Princeton University Press.

Becker, G. S. (1957), *The Economics of Discrimination*, Chicago, IL: Chicago University Press.

Becker, G. S. (1993), *Human Capital: A Theoretical and Empirical Analysis, with Special Reference to Education*, 3rd edn, Chicago, IL: Chicago University Press.

Becker, G. S. and B. R. Chiswick (1966), 'Education and the distribution of earnings', *American Economic Review*, 56: 358–69.

Bell, D. and F. Ritchie (1998), 'Female earnings and gender differentials in Great Britain 1977–1994', *Labour Economics*, 5(3): 331–57.

BERR (Department for Business Enterprise and Regulatory Reform) (2008) *Right to Request Flexible Working: A review of how to extend the right to request flexible working to parents of older children.*

Berthoud, R. (2006), *The Employment Rates of Disabled People*, Department for Work and Pensions Research Report 298.

Bjerk, D. (2008), 'Glass ceilings or sticky floors? Statistical discrimination in a dynamic model of hiring and promotion', *Economic Journal*, 118(530); 961–82.

Blau, F. D. and L. M. Kahn (1992), 'The gender earnings gap: learning from international comparisons', *American Economic Review*, May, pp. 533–8.

Blinder, A. L. (1973), 'Wage discrimination: reduced form and structural estimates', *Journal of Human Resources*, VIII: 436–55.

Booth, A. and J. C. van Ours (2008), 'Job satisfaction and family happiness: the part-time work puzzle', *Economic Journal*, 118(526): F77–F99.

Booth, A. L., J. Frank and D. Blackaby (2002), *Outside Offers and the Gender Pay Gap: Empirical Evidence from the UK Academic Labour Market*, Unpublished paper.

Chevalier, A. (2004), *Motivation, Expectations and the Gender Pay Gap for UK Graduates*, IZA Discussion Paper 1101.

Chevalier, A. (2007), 'Education, occupation and career expectations: determinants of the gender pay gap for UK graduates', *Oxford Bulletin of Economics and Statistics*, 69(6): 819–42.

Clarke, L., E. Frydendal Pederson, E. Michielsens, B. Susman and C. Wall (eds) (2004), *Women in Construction*, Reed Business Information.

Connolly, S. and M. Gregory (2007), 'Women and work since 1970', in *Work and Pay in Twentieth-century Britain*, Oxford: Oxford University Press, pp. 142–77.

Connolly, S. and M. Gregory (2008), 'Moving down: women's part-time work and occupational change in Britain 1991–2001', *Economic Journal*, 118(526): F52–F76.

Conservative Party (2007), *Fair Play on Women's Pay: A six point plan to overcome the gender pay gap*.

Daniels, H. (2008), 'Patterns of pay: results of the Annual Survey of Hours and Earnings 1997 to 2007', *Economic and Labour Market Review*, 2(2): 23–31.

Davies, R., R. Gilhooly and P. Jones (2007), *What Price Risk: Evidence of Compensating Differentials for the UK*, Unpublished paper, Swansea University.

Epstein, R. A. (1992), *Forbidden Grounds: The Case against Employment Discrimination Laws*, Cambridge, MA: Harvard University Press.

European Commission (2004), *Undeclared Work in an Enlarged Union*, Brussels.

European Commission (2007), *Discrimination in the European Union: Special Eurobarometer*, Brussels.

European Foundation for the Improvement of Living and Working Conditions (2006), *The Gender Pay Gap: Background Paper*, Dublin.

Eurostat (2008), *The Life of Women and Men in Europe: A statistical portrait*, Brussels: European Commission.

Goldin, C. and C. Rouse (2000), 'Orchestrating impartiality: the impact of "blind" auditions on female musicians', *American Economic Review*, 90(4): 715–41.

Grazier, S. (2007), *Compensating Wage Differentials for Risk of Death in Great Britain: An Examination of the Trade Union and Health and Safety Committee Impact*, Unpublished paper, Swansea University.

Gregory, M. and S. Connolly (2008), 'The price of reconciliation: part-time work, families and women's satisfaction', *Economic Journal*, 118(526): F1–F7.

Grimshaw, D. and J. Rubery (2002), *The Adjusted Gender Pay Gap: A critical appraisal of standard decomposition techniques*, Report prepared for the Group of Experts on Gender and Employment, Equal Opportunities Unit, European Commission.

Hakim, C. (2000), *Work–Lifestyle Choices in the 21st Century: Preference Theory*, Oxford: Oxford University Press.

Hakim, C. (2002) *Do Lifestyle Preferences Explain the Pay Gap?*, Paper presented to the Gender Research Forum.

Hakim, C., K. Bradley, E. Price and L. Mitchell (2008), *Little Britons: Financing Childcare Choice*, London: Policy Exchange.

Harkness, S. (1996) 'The gender earnings gap: evidence from the UK', *Fiscal Studies*, 17(2): 1–36.

Heckman, J. (1979), 'Sample selection bias as a specification error', *Econometrica*, 47: 153–61.

Henderson, D (1986), *Innocence and Design: The Influence of Economic Ideas on Policy*, Oxford: Basil Blackwell.

Holmes, S. (2008), 'Smashing the glass ceiling', BBC website.

House of Commons Business, Enterprise and Regulatory Reform Committee (2008), *Jobs for the Girls: Two Years On*.

House of Commons Trade and Industry Committee (2005), *Jobs for the Girls: The effect of occupational segregation on the gender pay gap*.

Hunt, J. (2002), 'The transition in East Germany: when is a ten-point fall in the gender wage gap bad news?', *Journal of Labor Economics*, 20: 148–69.

Institute for Fiscal Studies (2006), *The Effect of the Working Families' Tax Credit on Labour Market Participation*.

ITUC (International Trade Union Confederation) (2008), *The Global Gender Pay Gap*, Brussels.

Juhn, C., K. Murphy and B. Pierce (1991), 'Accounting for the slowdown in black–white wage convergence', in M. Kosters (ed.), *Workers and Their Wages*, Washington, DC: AEI Press.

Leaker, D. (2008), 'The gender pay gap in the UK', *Economic and Labour Market Review*, 2(4): 19–24.

Loewenthal, K. M., A. K. MacLeod and M. Cinnirella (2002), 'Are women more religious than men? Gender differences in religious activity among different religious groups in the UK', *Personality and Individual Differences*, 32(1): 133–9.

McNabb, R. (1989), 'Compensating wage differentials: some evidence for Britain', *Oxford Economic Papers*, 41: 327–38.

Manning, A. and B. Petrongolo (2008), 'The part-time penalty for women in Britain', *Economic Journal*, 118(526): F28–F51.

Manning, A. and J. Swaffield (2008), 'The gender gap in early-career wage growth', *Economic Journal*, 118(530): 983–1024.

Meager, N. and D. Hill (2005), *The Labour Market Participation and Employment of Disabled People in the UK*, Institute for Employment Studies Working Paper WP1.

Moorhead, J. (2004), 'For decades we've been told Sweden is a great place to be a working parent. But we've been duped', *Guardian*, 22 September.

Neumark, D. (1988), 'Employers' discrimination behaviour and the estimation of wage discrimination', *Journal of Human Resources*, 23: 279–95.

Oaxaca, R. (1973), 'Male–female wage differentials in urban labour markets', *International Economic Review*, 14: 693–709.

OECD (2002), *Employment Outlook*, OECD: Paris.

OECD (2008), *Employment Outlook*, OECD: Paris.

Olsen, W. and S. Walby (2004), *Modelling Gender Pay Gaps*, Working Paper Series no. 17, Equal Opportunities Commission.

Paull, G. (2008), 'Children and women's hours of work', *Economic Journal*, 118(526): F8–F27.

Phelps, E. (1972), 'The statistical theory of racism and sexism', *American Economic Review*, 62: 659–61.

Plantenga, J. and C. Remery (2006), *The Gender Pay Gap. Origins and policy responses*, Report prepared for the Equality Unit, European Commission.

Platt, L. (2006), *Pay Gaps: The Position of Ethnic Minority Women and Men*, Equal Opportunities Commission.

Polachek, S. W. and W. S. Siebert (1993), *The Economics of Earnings*, Cambridge: Cambridge University Press.

Polachek, S. W. and J. Xiang (2006), *The Gender Pay Gap: A Cross-Country Analysis*, Unpublished.

Preston, A. (2003), 'Gender earnings and PT pay in Australia', *British Journal of Industrial Relations*, 41(3): 417–33.

Pricewaterhousecoopers LLP (2005), *The Economic Benefits to Higher Education Qualifications: A Report for the Royal Society of Chemistry*.

Record, N. (2006), *Sir Humphrey's Legacy: Facing up to the cost of public sector pensions*, Hobart Paper 156, London: Institute of Economic Affairs.

Reeves, R. (2008), 'Work isn't working', *New Statesman*, 19 March.

Sealy, R., V. Singh and S. Vinnicombe (2007), *The Female FTSE Report 2007*, Cranfield University.

Simon, A. and E. Whiting (2007), 'Using the FRS to examine employment trends of couples', *Economic and Labour Market Review*, 1(11): 41–7.

Trendence (2008), *UK Graduate Recruitment Review 2008*.

TUC (2007), *Closing the Gender Pay Gap: An update report for TUC Women's Conference 2008*.

Weller, P., A. Feldman and K. Purdam (2001), *Religious Discrimination in England and Wales*, Home Office Research Study 220.

Women and Work Commission (2006), *Shaping a Fairer Future*.

ABOUT THE IEA

The Institute is a research and educational charity (No. CC 235 351), limited by guarantee. Its mission is to improve understanding of the fundamental institutions of a free society by analysing and expounding the role of markets in solving economic and social problems.

The IEA achieves its mission by:

- a high-quality publishing programme
- conferences, seminars, lectures and other events
- outreach to school and college students
- brokering media introductions and appearances

The IEA, which was established in 1955 by the late Sir Antony Fisher, is an educational charity, not a political organisation. It is independent of any political party or group and does not carry on activities intended to affect support for any political party or candidate in any election or referendum, or at any other time. It is financed by sales of publications, conference fees and voluntary donations.

In addition to its main series of publications the IEA also publishes a quarterly journal, *Economic Affairs*.

The IEA is aided in its work by a distinguished international Academic Advisory Council and an eminent panel of Honorary Fellows. Together with other academics, they review prospective IEA publications, their comments being passed on anonymously to authors. All IEA papers are therefore subject to the same rigorous independent refereeing process as used by leading academic journals.

IEA publications enjoy widespread classroom use and course adoptions in schools and universities. They are also sold throughout the world and often translated/reprinted.

Since 1974 the IEA has helped to create a worldwide network of 100 similar institutions in over 70 countries. They are all independent but share the IEA's mission.

Views expressed in the IEA's publications are those of the authors, not those of the Institute (which has no corporate view), its Managing Trustees, Academic Advisory Council members or senior staff.

Members of the Institute's Academic Advisory Council, Honorary Fellows, Trustees and Staff are listed on the following page.

The Institute gratefully acknowledges financial support for its publications programme and other work from a generous benefaction by the late Alec and Beryl Warren.

Other papers recently published by the IEA include:

WHO, What and Why?
Transnational Government, Legitimacy and the World Health Organization
Roger Scruton
Occasional Paper 113; ISBN 0 255 36487 3; £8.00

The World Turned Rightside Up
A New Trading Agenda for the Age of Globalisation
John C. Hulsman
Occasional Paper 114; ISBN 0 255 36495 4; £8.00

The Representation of Business in English Literature
Introduced and edited by Arthur Pollard
Readings 53; ISBN 0 255 36491 1; £12.00

Anti-Liberalism 2000
The Rise of New Millennium Collectivism
David Henderson
Occasional Paper 115; ISBN 0 255 36497 0; £7.50

Capitalism, Morality and Markets
Brian Griffiths, Robert A. Sirico, Norman Barry & Frank Field
Readings 54; ISBN 0 255 36496 2; £7.50

A Conversation with Harris and Seldon
Ralph Harris & Arthur Seldon
Occasional Paper 116; ISBN 0 255 36498 9; £7.50

Malaria and the DDT Story
Richard Tren & Roger Bate
Occasional Paper 117; ISBN 0 255 36499 7; £10.00

A Plea to Economists Who Favour Liberty: Assist the Everyman
Daniel B. Klein
Occasional Paper 118; ISBN 0 255 36501 2; £10.00

The Changing Fortunes of Economic Liberalism
Yesterday, Today and Tomorrow
David Henderson
Occasional Paper 105 (new edition); ISBN 0 255 36520 9; £12.50

The Global Education Industry
Lessons from Private Education in Developing Countries
James Tooley
Hobart Paper 141 (new edition); ISBN 0 255 36503 9; £12.50

Saving Our Streams
*The Role of the Anglers' Conservation Association in
Protecting English and Welsh Rivers*
Roger Bate
Research Monograph 53; ISBN 0 255 36494 6; £10.00

Better Off Out?
The Benefits or Costs of EU Membership
Brian Hindley & Martin Howe
Occasional Paper 99 (new edition); ISBN 0 255 36502 0; £10.00

Buckingham at 25
Freeing the Universities from State Control
Edited by James Tooley
Readings 55; ISBN 0 255 36512 8; £15.00

Lectures on Regulatory and Competition Policy
Irwin M. Stelzer
Occasional Paper 120; ISBN 0 255 36511 X; £12.50

Misguided Virtue
False Notions of Corporate Social Responsibility
David Henderson
Hobart Paper 142; ISBN 0 255 36510 1; £12.50

HIV and Aids in Schools
The Political Economy of Pressure Groups and Miseducation
Barrie Craven, Pauline Dixon, Gordon Stewart & James Tooley
Occasional Paper 121; ISBN 0 255 36522 5; £10.00

The Road to Serfdom
The Reader's Digest *condensed version*
Friedrich A. Hayek
Occasional Paper 122; ISBN 0 255 36530 6; £7.50

Bastiat's *The Law*
Introduction by Norman Barry
Occasional Paper 123; ISBN 0 255 36509 8; £7.50

A Globalist Manifesto for Public Policy
Charles Calomiris
Occasional Paper 124; ISBN 0 255 36525 x; £7.50

Euthanasia for Death Duties
Putting Inheritance Tax Out of Its Misery
Barry Bracewell-Milnes
Research Monograph 54; ISBN 0 255 36513 6; £10.00

Liberating the Land
The Case for Private Land-use Planning
Mark Pennington
Hobart Paper 143; ISBN 0 255 36508 x; £10.00

IEA Yearbook of Government Performance 2002/2003
Edited by Peter Warburton
Yearbook 1; ISBN 0 255 36532 2; £15.00

Britain's Relative Economic Performance, 1870–1999
Nicholas Crafts
Research Monograph 55; ISBN 0 255 36524 1; £10.00

Should We Have Faith in Central Banks?
Otmar Issing
Occasional Paper 125; ISBN 0 255 36528 4; £7.50

The Dilemma of Democracy
Arthur Seldon
Hobart Paper 136 (reissue); ISBN 0 255 36536 5; £10.00

Capital Controls: a 'Cure' Worse Than the Problem?
Forrest Capie
Research Monograph 56; ISBN 0 255 36506 3; £10.00

The Poverty of 'Development Economics'
Deepak Lal
Hobart Paper 144 (reissue); ISBN 0 255 36519 5; £15.00

Should Britain Join the Euro?
The Chancellor's Five Tests Examined
Patrick Minford
Occasional Paper 126; ISBN 0 255 36527 6; £7.50

Post-Communist Transition: Some Lessons
Leszek Balcerowicz
Occasional Paper 127; ISBN 0 255 36533 0; £7.50

A Tribute to Peter Bauer
John Blundell et al.
Occasional Paper 128; ISBN 0 255 36531 4; £10.00

Employment Tribunals
Their Growth and the Case for Radical Reform
J. R. Shackleton
Hobart Paper 145; ISBN 0 255 36515 2; £10.00

Fifty Economic Fallacies Exposed
Geoffrey E. Wood
Occasional Paper 129; ISBN 0 255 36518 7; £12.50

Economy and Virtue
Essays on the Theme of Markets and Morality
Edited by Dennis O'Keeffe
Readings 59; ISBN 0 255 36504 7; £12.50

Free Markets Under Siege
Cartels, Politics and Social Welfare
Richard A. Epstein
Occasional Paper 132; ISBN 0 255 36553 5; £10.00

Unshackling Accountants
D. R. Myddelton
Hobart Paper 149; ISBN 0 255 36559 4; £12.50

The Euro as Politics
Pedro Schwartz
Research Monograph 58; ISBN 0 255 36535 7; £12.50

Pricing Our Roads
Vision and Reality
Stephen Glaister & Daniel J. Graham
Research Monograph 59; ISBN 0 255 36562 4; £10.00

The Role of Business in the Modern World
Progress, Pressures, and Prospects for the Market Economy
David Henderson
Hobart Paper 150; ISBN 0 255 36548 9; £12.50

Public Service Broadcasting Without the BBC?
Alan Peacock
Occasional Paper 133; ISBN 0 255 36565 9; £10.00

The ECB and the Euro: the First Five Years
Otmar Issing
Occasional Paper 134; ISBN 0 255 36555 1; £10.00

Towards a Liberal Utopia?
Edited by Philip Booth
Hobart Paperback 32; ISBN 0 255 36563 2; £15.00

The Way Out of the Pensions Quagmire
Philip Booth & Deborah Cooper
Research Monograph 60; ISBN 0 255 36517 9; £12.50

Black Wednesday
A Re-examination of Britain's Experience in the Exchange Rate Mechanism
Alan Budd
Occasional Paper 135; ISBN 0 255 36566 7; £7.50

Crime: Economic Incentives and Social Networks
Paul Ormerod
Hobart Paper 151; ISBN 0 255 36554 3; £10.00

The Road to Serfdom *with* **The Intellectuals and Socialism**
Friedrich A. Hayek
Occasional Paper 136; ISBN 0 255 36576 4; £10.00

Money and Asset Prices in Boom and Bust
Tim Congdon
Hobart Paper 152; ISBN 0 255 36570 5; £10.00

The Dangers of Bus Re-regulation
and Other Perspectives on Markets in Transport
John Hibbs et al.
Occasional Paper 137; ISBN 0 255 36572 1; £10.00

The New Rural Economy
Change, Dynamism and Government Policy
Berkeley Hill et al.
Occasional Paper 138; ISBN 0 255 36546 2; £15.00

The Benefits of Tax Competition
Richard Teather
Hobart Paper 153; ISBN 0 255 36569 1; £12.50

Wheels of Fortune
Self-funding Infrastructure and the Free Market Case for a Land Tax
Fred Harrison
Hobart Paper 154; ISBN 0 255 36589 6; £12.50

Were 364 Economists All Wrong?
Edited by Philip Booth
Readings 60; ISBN 978 0 255 36588 8; £10.00

Europe After the 'No' Votes
Mapping a New Economic Path
Patrick A. Messerlin
Occasional Paper 139; ISBN 978 0 255 36580 2; £10.00

The Railways, the Market and the Government
John Hibbs et al.
Readings 61; ISBN 978 0 255 36567 3; £12.50

Corruption: The World's Big C
Cases, Causes, Consequences, Cures
Ian Senior
Research Monograph 61; ISBN 978 0 255 36571 0; £12.50

Choice and the End of Social Housing
Peter King
Hobart Paper 155; ISBN 978 0 255 36568 0; £10.00

Sir Humphrey's Legacy
Facing Up to the Cost of Public Sector Pensions
Neil Record
Hobart Paper 156; ISBN 978 0 255 36578 9; £10.00

The Economics of Law
Cento Veljanovski
Second edition
Hobart Paper 157; ISBN 978 0 255 36561 1; £12.50

Living with Leviathan
Public Spending, Taxes and Economic Performance
David B. Smith
Hobart Paper 158; ISBN 978 0 255 36579 6; £12.50

The Vote Motive
Gordon Tullock
New edition
Hobart Paperback 33; ISBN 978 0 255 36577 2; £10.00

Waging the War of Ideas
John Blundell
Third edition
Occasional Paper 131; ISBN 978 0 255 36606 9; £12.50

The War Between the State and the Family
How Government Divides and Impoverishes
Patricia Morgan
Hobart Paper 159; ISBN 978 0 255 36596 3; £10.00

Capitalism – A Condensed Version
Arthur Seldon
Occasional Paper 140; ISBN 978 0 255 36598 7; £7.50

Catholic Social Teaching and the Market Economy
Edited by Philip Booth
Hobart Paperback 34; ISBN 978 0 255 36581 9; £15.00

Adam Smith – A Primer
Eamonn Butler
Occasional Paper 141; ISBN 978 0 255 36608 3; £7.50

Happiness, Economics and Public Policy
Helen Johns & Paul Ormerod
Research Monograph 62; ISBN 978 0 255 36600 7; £10.00

They Meant Well
Government Project Disasters
D. R. Myddelton
Hobart Paper 160; ISBN 978 0 255 36601 4; £12.50

Rescuing Social Capital from Social Democracy
John Meadowcroft & Mark Pennington
Hobart Paper 161; ISBN 978 0 255 36592 5; £10.00

Paths to Property
Approaches to Institutional Change in International Development
Karol Boudreaux & Paul Dragos Aligica
Hobart Paper 162; ISBN 978 0 255 36582 6; £10.00

Prohibitions
Edited by John Meadowcroft
Hobart Paperback 35; ISBN 978 0 255 36585 7; £15.00

Trade Policy, New Century
The WTO, FTAs and Asia Rising
Razeen Sally
Hobart Paper 163; ISBN 978 0 255 36544 4; £12.50

Sixty Years On – Who Cares for the NHS?
Helen Evans
Research Monograph 63; ISBN 978 0 255 36611 3; £10.00

Taming Leviathan
Waging the War of Ideas Around the World
Edited by Colleen Dyble
Occasional Paper 142; ISBN 978 0 255 36607 6; £12.50

The Legal Foundations of Free Markets
Edited by Stephen F. Copp
Hobart Paperback 36; ISBN 978 0 255 36591 8; £15.00

Climate Change Policy: Challenging the Activists
Edited by Colin Robinson
Readings 62; ISBN 978 0 255 36595 6; £10.00

Other IEA publications

Comprehensive information on other publications and the wider work of the IEA can be found at www.iea.org.uk. To order any publication please see below.

Personal and academic customers

Orders from personal and academic customers should be directed to the IEA:

Bob Layson
IEA
2 Lord North Street
FREEPOST LON10168
London SW1P 3YZ
Tel: 020 7799 8909. Fax: 020 7799 2137
Email: blayson@iea.org.uk

Trade customers

All orders from the book trade should be directed to the IEA's distributor:

Gazelle Book Services Ltd (IEA Orders)
FREEPOST RLYS-EAHU-YSCZ
White Cross Mills
Hightown
Lancaster LA1 4XS
Tel: 01524 68765, Fax: 01524 53232
Email: sales@gazellebooks.co.uk

IEA subscriptions

The IEA also offers a subscription service to its publications. For a single annual payment (currently £42.00 in the UK), subscribers receive every monograph the IEA publishes. For more information please contact:

Adam Myers
Subscriptions
IEA
2 Lord North Street
FREEPOST LON10168
London SW1P 3YZ
Tel: 020 7799 8920, Fax: 020 7799 2137
Email: amyers@iea.org.uk